PRAISE FOR
PARENTING ATHLETIC KIDS

"Travis provides real-life advice backed by the knowledge of education, his own career, and his own parenting. As someone who is involved in several youth baseball programs, what he says about *Parenting Athletic Kids* is absolute gospel. Parents should take to heart the knowledge and wisdom provided in this book to raise their own sons or daughters."

— Greg Reinhard
Former Tampa Bay Ray and Chicago Cub
Founder - GRB Academy and the GRB Rays

"Two years ago, I struggled as a father with coaching my son in baseball. I did not know how to control my emotions and it wore on the relationship with my son. This was all on me, but it affected both of us. On the field, in the dugout, car rides home, etc. I had seen a family friend post online about MindRite Training and this guy who helped young athletes and parents with the mental side of sports. I never knew mental training for young athletes existed. Fast forward: after my son and I both worked with Travis, we are happy to call Travis a trusted friend. He has helped both of us with ways to prepare, adapt, and reflect on different aspects in sports, and more importantly, ways we can incorporate this into everyday life. Reading *Parenting Athletic Kids* recently reinforces so many of the topics that I can incorporate into relationships with my son, my daughter, and the other young athletes I coach. Focusing on controllables, process over outcome, and next pitch mindset;

these are all huge components of having the best opportunity of success, and enjoying the process altogether.

The support I give to my kids and their friends in sports/life has not been perfect. There have definitely been some peaks and valleys over the past two years. And I know that will continue. But for my son and I both, I know that this is a journey with no shortcuts. I am proud to call Travis a friend of our family, and that my son has developed a relationship with someone he can trust to have these conversations with Travis. I cannot wait to have a hard copy of this book with 'post-it' flags hanging out of the pages."

— Dan Slepica

"Sports have been in our family's life from the moment our kids could participate. Like many parents, we enjoyed making new friends. We enjoyed watching our kids enjoy a game they loved with friends they loved. And like our kids, we love competition. The knowledge of the growth mindset, the sports and athletic mental approach, and the goal setting has not only helped our children, but us as parents. Controllable goals both short term and long term filter in our conversations with our young adult children.

Our son and daughter were gifted Coach Rogers during their formative years of youth sports. Both have had injury setbacks, times when the grind might have seemed like too much, and have experienced their share of "bad calls." Phrases like "Be the Best Teammate," "Trust the Process," and "Next Pitch!" have dominated their lives through their past 11 years of sports. "Control what you can Control" became a life lesson Senior Season of 2020.

If you are looking for a way to grow your relationship with your youth athlete, Coach Rogers' book is for you.

If you are wondering if there is a guiding handbook on how to embrace the lessons sports can teach, Coach Rogers' book is for you.

If you are looking for a way to enjoy your athletes' competition, knowing that a win on the field is a goal, but growth is the long game, then Coach Rogers' book is for you.

The games seem long, but the seasons are short. Enjoy to the fullest!"

— Laura Bateman

"Travis' methods and ideas have been invaluable to both of my boys in their athletic journey. The basketball teams I have coached through the years have worked directly with Travis and achieved tangible success on the court and off the court in that process. But the methods that Travis teaches have been a gift to me as a parent as well. I've used Travis' ideas to ask our sons, "What did you do well?" or "What would you like to improve on?" after almost every game they have played. But his greatest gift to me as a parent was his reminder to tell my sons "I love watching you play," as much as I can…"

— Steve Weber

"*Parenting Athletic Kids* is an extremely valuable read for parents that want to be involved in providing a positive and lasting experience for their sons and daughters through their athletics. One of the most important values of sports is developing character in our young people. Parents can have tremendous influence on this character development through their child's athletic experiences. This book provides a blueprint for parents to be actively involved! Having coached with Travis Rogers for several years, I know firsthand that his dedication and insight into the athlete's character development as both a Coach and a Parent is exceptional!"

— Mark Downey,
Head Baseball Coach Mounds View High School, MN

"Travis has written a guide for parents navigating the challenging and ever-changing world of youth sports. This book is not just a playbook; it's a compass, providing direction in creating an environment that promotes the development of confident, resilient, and hardworking young athletes.

With a blend of wisdom and practical advice, Travis tackles the intricacies of parenting a youth athlete, offering a blueprint for establishing an environment for growth and success. He combines personal anecdotes with actionable strategies, ensuring that every chapter is not only informative but also engaging. *Parenting Athletic Kids* is a timely resource for parents hoping to maintain the appropriate balance between support and empowerment.

Whether you're a seasoned sports parent or just stepping into this scene, Travis provides insights that will resonate. *Parenting Athletic Kids* is a must-read for anyone committed to nurturing the holistic development of their young athlete."

— Brian Bambenek, Owner,
Great Lakes Baseball Academy

PARENTING
ATHLETIC KIDS

Creating the Optimal Environment
for Confidence, Resilience, and Work Ethic

PARENTING ATHLETIC KIDS

Creating the Optimal Environment
for Confidence, Resilience, and Work Ethic

TRAVIS ROGERS

Parenting Athletic Kids: Creating the Optimal Environment for Confidence, Resilience, and Work Ethic

Copyright © 2024 by Travis Rogers

All rights reserved. No part of this publication may be reproduced, distributed, or transmitted in any form or by any means, including photocopying, recording, or other electronic or mechanical methods, without the prior written permission of the author, except in the case of brief quotations embodied in critical reviews and certain other noncommercial uses permitted by copyright law.

Jones Media Publishing
10645 N. Tatum Blvd. Ste. 200-166
Phoenix, AZ 85028
JonesMediaPublishing.com

Disclaimer:

The author strives to be as accurate and complete as possible in the creation of this book, notwithstanding the fact that the author does not warrant or represent at any time that the contents within are accurate due to the rapidly changing nature of the Internet. While all attempts have been made to verify information provided in this publication, the Author and the Publisher assume no responsibility and are not liable for errors, omissions, or contrary interpretation of the subject matter herein. The Author and Publisher hereby disclaim any liability, loss or damage incurred as a result of the application and utilization, whether directly or indirectly, of any information, suggestion, advice, or procedure in this book. Any perceived slights of specific persons, peoples, or organizations are unintentional.

Printed in the United States of America

ISBN: 978-1-948382-85-4 paperback

FREE READER BONUS

Discover the 3 Keys To Optimal Health For Young Athletes

Free training to enjoy for yourself, or with your kids:

mindritetraining.com/parentingathletickids

I would like to thank my dad for his level headedness and unwavering support. I would also like to thank my wife, Nancy, for her huge heart and her relentless desire to raise two fine young men. A big shoutout to all the coaches I have ever had the honor of taking the field with. Without you and your wisdom, this book, and my life, would be incomplete. And last, but certainly not least, my two boys, Will and Drew. Through the two of you I was able to rekindle a lost love for sports and specifically baseball. I am so proud of the men you have become.

TABLE OF CONTENTS

Foreword xv

Chapter 1: The Optimal Sports Experience 1

Chapter 2: My Journey. 5

Chapter 3: Growth Mindset 7

Chapter 4: Enjoyment 15

Chapter 5: Athletic Development 19

Chapter 6: Personal Development 27

Chapter 7: Journaling. 49

Chapter 8: Age-Specific Considerations. 59

Chapter 9: Dealing With Pressure 69

Chapter 10: Trophies For Everyone!. 89

Chapter 11: Coaching Your Son or Daughter 93

Chapter 12: Final Thoughts 101

Reference Guide 103

About The Author 105

FOREWORD

"Failure is inevitable, take chances"

— Lucie Henrich,
Gustavus Adolphus, Soccer

Do sports build character, or reveal it?

I often hear this question with regard to sports. Some say participation in youth sports builds character: work ethic, confidence, teamwork, compassion. Others say sports reveal character: competitiveness, resilience, accountability. I believe sports can build character traits, sometimes good traits and sometimes bad, and reveal the traits that have already been built.

There are athletes throughout sports that have good character traits (high character) and there are athletes that have bad character traits (low character), so it can't be sports in and of themselves that create high- or low-character individuals. What about specific sports? Does baseball have all high-character athletes? Does basketball have all low-character athletes? Hockey? Football? You can find high- and low-character athletes in every sport. What builds high-character individuals is a focused effort to build high-character individuals. If we want our son to become more resilient, we focus our attention on building his resiliency. If we want our daughter to have a great work ethic, we focus on teaching her the benefits of hard work.

That's right—parents <u>must</u> play a lead role in the successful development of high-character individuals. A key value of sports is that they challenge many of the character traits we want our sons and daughters to acquire. Traits like work ethic, resilience, confidence, and accountability are tested all the time in sports. It is our responsibility as parents to help prepare them for these tests. The side benefit is that all the character traits built through sports will transfer to other kinds of tests off the field: life's tests in school, relationships, and work.

This book is all about preparing today's youth athletes for the tests—the tests in sports, and the tests in life. Yes, we parents play a role in that preparation; we can help, but also potentially hinder that preparation. The result of our parental involvement can be to help build high-character individuals...or low-character ones.

At the end of the day, our son or daughter's athletic achievements are not a reflection of the job we have done raising a young athlete. Rather, it is our son or daughter's character that reflects the job we have done.

CHAPTER 1

THE OPTIMAL SPORTS EXPERIENCE

"I believe that it's crucial for young players to find passion in their sport. During my early days in club sports, I played purely for the enjoyment of the game. However, as I transitioned into more competitive play, and the stakes increased with recruitment, I found myself setting exceptionally high standards. At times, this led to a strained relationship with lacrosse, swinging between moments of joy and frustration."

— Olivia Kingsborough,
Boston University, Lacrosse

I hope this book works as a resource for you, the parent, in your quest to provide an optimal sports experience for your child. This book can serve as a blueprint to help navigate the ups and downs that are inherent in youth sports. It can provide a guide to help you steer your young athlete toward a mindset that will not only heighten their sports experience, but will also benefit them both on and off the playing field. I also hope this book helps you, the parent, enjoy the ride.

The landscape of youth sports has changed dramatically over the last several years. Club sports, specialization, and one-on-one training are now the norm. Pressure to perform based on outcomes (highlighted by social media platforms) has changed our perception of sports. A shift has occurred: away from sports being fun, a way to get exercise, and a way to develop good people, and toward a focus on being the best, earning a scholarship, or making it to the professional ranks. This shift has caused emotional strain on both the athlete and the parent.

I have written this book to ease the emotional strain. This book gives a step-by-step guide to help you, and your son or daughter, navigate the current sports landscape and get the most out of the experience.

What defines the optimal sports experience? The optimal sports experience can be broken into three essential categories: Enjoyment, Athletic Development, and Personal Development.

Enjoyment

Above all else, it is essential that the youth athlete enjoy their sport. They should enjoy their time on the field, ice, court, etc. They should make new friends, laugh, smile, and have fun at practices and in games. Without fun, what is the point? Without fun, how long will it last?

I spoke to a client recently who is a junior in high school. When we began working together, during his sophomore year, he was stressed because he didn't feel like he was getting enough playing time. He feared that this lack of playing time would affect his chances of being recruited by a Division 1 school. Playing Division 1 basketball had been his dream for as long as he can remember. A few months after our initial conversation I spoke to him again. He was doing really well. He was playing with his summer Amateur Athletic Union (AAU) basketball team, and multiple Division 1 schools were showing interest in him. When I spoke to him again recently, he was very discouraged. He told me he had lost his desire to play. The passion was gone. The stress and anxiety of the process had worn him down.

So how did it come to this? He couldn't put his finger on exactly when it happened, but at some point he just stopped having fun. The game he had played with love and passion had become a chore.

Without finding joy through the game, the passion will fade. As parents, we should place enjoyment of the sport experience above everything else. People often ask me how my oldest son, who is very passionate about baseball, fell so deeply in love with his sport. For me, it is simple: he has always had fun.

Athletic Development

The father of a 12-year-old baseball player asked a pitching coach for an off-season training program for his son. The father wanted the same training program that the pitching coach had given to a professional player. The coach then asked the father if he wanted the program that the professional was doing when he was 12. The dad said no; he wanted the program that the professional was doing right now. The coach told the father that his 12-year-old son was not ready for a professional's program. The father then told the coach that he would take his business elsewhere.

Does this story seem far-fetched? Maybe a little crazy? It's a true story. We all want the best development for our young athletes. If we are going to invest our time and our money, the performance of our young athletes should be getting better...right? Yes, but there is so much more.

Personal Development

Teamwork. Overcoming mistakes. Confidence. Leadership. Sports can help build these great character traits and many more.

But are these traits going to be built just because we sign up our kids for sports? No chance. We as parents need to play a role in the development of these traits. If we are not careful, we can even play a role in reducing the development of these positive traits. What?! How might I negatively impact the development of good character traits as a parent?

Here is an example. I discuss "controlling what you can control" with athletes. They must learn to take ownership of their thoughts. If they allow elements outside of their control to infiltrate their thoughts, they forfeit control of their development. A great example of this is how parents deal with umpires. If young athletes allow an umpire to affect their thoughts (e.g. by getting frustrated with a tough call) they are not "controlling what they can control." I go through this concept over and over with players. The players get it and are generally fantastic about controlling their thoughts regarding umpires. Then the following scenario arises: 10-year-old Timmy strikes out looking on a pitch that was 4 inches outside. Timmy's dad begins hollering at the umpire. Dad is now sending a message to Timmy, and everyone around him, that it is okay for Timmy to lose control of his thoughts. Dad is saying that it is okay to let uncontrollable influences control Timmy's thoughts. This is just one example of how we as parents can impact our sons' and daughters' character development.

Enjoyment, athletic development, and their interrelationship with personal development will be covered in greater detail later in the book.

CHAPTER 2

MY JOURNEY

"Focus on your own journey"

— *Lucie Henrich,*
Gustavus Adolphus, Soccer

I played multiple sports growing up: soccer, basketball, football, and baseball. Like most, my parents would drop me off at my sporting event and go about their business. Although I enjoyed all sports, I really loved baseball, probably because it was the sport I was best at. I grew up in New York City and dreamed of playing catcher for the Yankees. I played football and baseball in high school, and I earned "All Conference" and "All Metro" in baseball my senior season. Following high school, I played two seasons of Junior College baseball. In my first year, we made it to the Junior College World Series. In my sophomore year, we were only one game short of making it back to the Junior College World Series. After my two years at junior college, I went on to play Division 1 baseball at New Mexico State University. My first season at New Mexico State was great: we were led by a great group of seniors, we won a ton of games, and I had a blast. I played well that season, splitting time with a senior. Then came my senior season. It was my last chance to be seen. It was my last chance to get drafted. I knew I had to produce. I started feeling the pressure long before the season ever started. I was named team captain, and what should have been an honor just added more pressure. I was focused on my own production, and when I didn't produce, the pressure mounted. By the halfway point of the season, our team was losing most of our games, and I was playing terribly. I considered quitting. The game that I had loved for as long as I could remember had become a terrible grind. One of the coaches on the team urged me to stick it out, which I did, but after that terrible season I never played baseball again.

Fast forward twenty years. I was back on the field coaching my eight-year-old son, Will. I was really enjoying coaching his baseball team…enjoying almost everything about it. The only thing I was not enjoying was watching how hard the kids were on themselves when they made mistakes. They were easily frustrated, leading to tears and bad body language. I began to wonder <u>why</u> they were so hard on themselves. I don't remember ever crying after a strikeout. Their frustrations weren't just happening after a "big" team loss, which I could understand—they were happening all the time. I began to dig deeper, studying the mental side of the game. With this motivation, I went back to school, at age forty-five, and got my master's degree in Sport and Exercise Science with an emphasis in Sport Psychology.

Will is now twenty-one, a junior at the University of Michigan. Drew, our younger son, is eighteen, a senior in high school. I have been coaching for the past thirteen years. I have coached baseball from the tee ball level through the high school varsity level. I also coached football for six years at the youth level. I have opened a business, MindRite Training, working with athletes on their mental performance. Along the way I have had many successes and also many failures. I have learned much and I continue to learn. My goal in writing this book is to relate many of the lessons I have learned as a player, a coach, a student, and a parent.

CHAPTER 3

GROWTH MINDSET

"When I was eleven a coach told me to be the best at what I can do, not what others want me to do. That really opened me up towards the idea of having an open mind towards failure and being my own athlete."

— *Ben Rosin,*
Kansas State University, Baseball

When I coached 10U baseball, I had many players that would act poorly when something went wrong. They would throw their bats when they struck out. They would toss their gloves when they made an error. They would get mad at umpires. They would get frustrated with their teammates. They were prone to bad body language when things didn't go their way. And they would cry. They would cry when they struck out, grounded out, or flew out. I had one player in particular that absolutely hated it when he didn't have the success he desired. If he didn't get a hit, make all the plays, or pitch up to his standards, he was an absolute wreck.

This is when I started to really focus my attention on the mental side of the game. Why were these kids so hard on themselves? I started talking to them about controllable aspects of the game. I asked them questions. "Do you think you have 100% control of whether or not you get a hit?" To my surprise, most of them answered, "Yes!" Oh my...here was the problem: these young players had unrealistic expectations. They were trying to control things they could not control.

We began to have conversations about what they actually did and did not control. I said things like, "If we can control whether or not we get a hit, then why do the best players in the world only get a hit three out of ten times?" Or, "What if you do everything right? You absolutely smoke a ball right at the center fielder, but he catches it for an out. Should you be upset?" The guys began to come around. Their expectations changed. Yes, they still wanted to get hits, but they came to realize that their best chance of getting a hit was to focus on things they control: things like their preparation, timing up the pitcher, and taking their best swings.

The young man I mentioned earlier, the one that really struggled when he didn't have success, became one of the most even-tempered players I have ever coached. Never too high, never too low. He went on to play Division 1 baseball.

An athlete's experience in sports, both enjoyment and performance, starts with their mindset. Carol Dweck, a professor at Stanford University, has conducted extensive research on how people learn. Dweck has found two types of learners: "growth mindset" learners, and "fixed mindset" learners. Here are some of the traits of a "growth mindset" learner:

- Believes skills are built
- Focuses on the process
- Believes effort will lead to growth
- Embraces challenges
- Believes mistakes are an opportunity to learn
- Appreciates feedback

Here are some traits of a "fixed mindset" learner:

- Believes skills are born
- Focuses on the outcome
- Believes effort is not necessary
- Avoids challenges
- Believes mistakes should be avoided
- Takes feedback personally

I think it is worthwhile to take a second look at these two lists. Which mindset will lead to a better experience for your son or daughter? Certainly it is that of a "growth mindset" learner.

We want young athletes to believe that they can improve with focused practice. We want young athletes to know that hard work, overcoming adversity, and focusing on the process will lead them to be the best versions of themselves.

Given its importance, can young people develop a "growth mindset?" Absolutely! How does this happen? As parents, we *must* focus on the process (steps along the way) instead of the outcome (results). What does that mean? We should emphasize:

- Teamwork
- Effort
- Positive attitude
- Energy
- The ability to overcome adversity
- Good body language

If we emphasize these things, all of which are controllable, our young athlete will learn that he or she is in control of their progress.

Why is focusing on "controllables" so important? If we focus on results (hits, touchdowns, baskets, etc.), we are at the mercy of things outside of our control (umpire calls, the opposing team's pitcher, strong defensive plays, good or bad luck, etc.) that can control the results. If we place our emphasis on these uncontrollable factors, we ride a roller coaster of emotions, and lose sight of what is truly important: *that our own effort leads to the best possible overall results.* Focusing on uncontrollables also makes young athletes nervous. If they are concerned about how many hits they get, they are concerned about something outside of their control, and this leads to anxiety. Playing nervously is no fun and generally leads to reduced levels of performance.

If an athlete focuses on controllables, they are at ease with emotions. They know that if they give their best effort and focus on the process, they will give themselves the best chance of success. Not *guaranteed* success, but the *best chance* of success.

What is the "process?" The "process" is the learned set of controllable physical and mental techniques that are used leading up to and during games. I'll get into this in much more detail later, but an example of a physical technique would be a quality warm-up, and an example of a mental technique would be journaling before games.

Before moving on, let's circle back to the "growth mindset" factors that we must focus on if we are going to nurture a "growth mindset."

Process over outcome. We *must* focus our athlete's attention on the process and steer them away from the outcome (result). How do we do this? We applaud effort, energy, hustle, being a good teammate, work ethic, and how well they overcome mistakes. Again, this helps athletes relax, enjoy themselves, and play their best. If we focus on results, telling them how great they are when they go 4-4 at the plate in a baseball game, what happens when they go 0-4? Are we then disappointed? Have they let us down? Have they let themselves down? Can you see the problem here? They can put in just as much effort when they went 0-4 as they did when they went 4-4. Remember, we want them to know that effort is what they should value. Effort will lead to positive results. Focusing on effort will nurture a "growth mindset." Focusing on results will nurture a "fixed" mindset. This is *really* hard. I have struggled with this as much as anyone. We want to praise them when they get good results. We can still praise them, but what we should say when they do well is, "You have worked so hard; keep up the great work." When they have a tough game, we should say, "This is part of the process of growth; keep working hard." I know, it's easier said than done. I promise you: the more you do this, the easier and more natural it will become. As I have developed this with my sons, my level of enjoyment has gone way up. I am much less concerned with how my sons perform. My focus has shifted to the controllables and the process. I no longer see hits or strikeouts as a reflection of my worth as a parent. I only ask myself whether they are being great teammates, growing as players and people, and giving their best. This is a true *game changer*.

"We" over "Me." When athletes focus on personal results (which are generally out of their control), they get tense and don't perform their best. If they focus on being a great teammate, no matter the result, they can look back and feel like they contributed. Being a great teammate has the added benefit of inspiring extra support from teammates and coaches. All teammates and coaches want to support great teammates. Players that are selfish invariably lose that support. So, paradoxically, if an athlete wants to be their best, they should focus more on others and less on themselves. Teammates and coaches will push and support a great teammate. Teammates and coaches will walk away from a bad teammate. We must be sure to incentivize great teamwork. When our son or daughter does something that lifts up a member of their team, we must celebrate!

Effort. We must focus on and celebrate effort. Compliment the work they are putting in. Celebrate the diving attempt. Again, effort is controllable. We know that effort will lead to better outcomes. It is harder now than ever for young people to see the correlation between effort and results. The media focuses on the outcome and not the effort. Young people see athletes signing multi-million-dollar contracts, but don't see the effort that the athlete has put in. Young people are praised for outcomes: they get an A in school and are praised for being so smart, rather than for working so hard. They see things on social media that make them think anyone can have an amazing car and a huge house. It has simply become less and less obvious that it takes great effort to achieve one's true potential.

Attitude. Having a great attitude elevates everything. Again, this is 100% controllable. I know, some days it's easier than others, but isn't that the trick? It is an amazing player development skill and personal development skill to be aware of our attitude, and to make adjustments on it as necessary. We know that a great attitude will give us the best chance of growth. I ask my athletes to check in on their attitude prior to games and practices. I let them know that it may not always be the best and the brightest, but that they are in control of their attitude. Again, the ability to be aware of their attitude, and understand the importance of having a good attitude, can play a major role in their development both on and off the field. As parents, we can simply ask our athletes how their attitude is before practices and games. This opens up discussion and gets them thinking about a controllable and important aspect of their development.

Energy. Similar to attitude, certain levels of energy are needed to produce growth, and higher energy levels will then promote more growth. I like to equate this to exercise. If I work out with low levels of energy, how much will my health improve? If I work out with high levels of energy, how much will my health improve? It's a no-brainer that better energy equals better results. Similar to attitude, self-awareness is key. We don't always feel the most energetic, but if we are aware of times when our energy is low, and we understand the importance of good energy, we can make adjustments. This awareness can be driven by intentional mindfulness before practices and games. I have my athletes ask themselves the simple question, "How is my energy on a scale of one to ten?" I talk to athletes about the importance of trying to be as high on the scale as possible. They won't always be a nine or ten, but they can always dig a little deeper.

The ability to overcome adversity. This is HUGE for creating an environment that fosters fun, physical development, and personal development—and for creating a "growth mindset!" Yes, it is again 100% controllable, and one of the most important skills for an athlete to learn. It is not easy, but is invaluable in their growth. This once again starts with you, the parent. Do we lose our minds when our athlete makes a mistake? If we do, we are sending a "fixed mindset" message directly to the athlete. "You messed up." "You're no good." "You let us down." "You let your team down." "You let yourself down." This is what an athlete hears when we get upset when they make a mistake. Sad, but true. Instead, this is a time to be supportive. "Get the next one." "Next pitch." "Keep working hard." "Your teammates have your back." These are the words we should be saying. We need an athlete to know that a mistake is simply an opportunity to learn and grow, to ask themselves, "What can I do better or differently?" Of course, sometimes they can be doing everything right and it will still not go their way! Trust me, young athletes beat themselves up enough. We need to support them, not undercut them. Use your words and body language to show your support when mistakes are made.

I was coaching third base during one of Will's games. Will was up to bat and took a pitch right down the middle. I didn't say anything, but I was frustrated. Will proceeded to have bad body language during the rest of the at-bat. After the game, I talked to him about his body language. "Your body language was terrible after you took that strike down the middle. You need to get over it, and move to the next pitch." "Dad, it was hard for me to get over it because you slumped over and put your hands on your knees like you were disgusted," he responded. Wow. Sorry, son.

Good body language. And that leads us right into body language. Again, this is 100% controllable. Good body language can lead to improved thinking. Often we think we must have a great attitude and great energy to have great body language, but the opposite can be true. Pull your shoulders back and sit up straight. Does that elevate your energy? I have read many stories about top athletes who improve their body language to improve their energy. Our young athletes should know about this. They should also understand that their body language can affect others as much as it affects themselves. Bad body language can affect the entire team. We should convey the importance of good body language to our athletes. It can change the game for them and their team.

In the next three chapters I will circle back to the three main factors in the athlete's optimal sport experience: Enjoyment, athletic development, and personal development.

CHAPTER 4

ENJOYMENT

"Despite the ongoing highs and lows of my lacrosse journey, having my parents there to provide support and listen to what I have to say makes it much easier to navigate through the challenging days."

— Olivia Kingsborough,
Boston University, Lacrosse

As I stated earlier, our children's enjoyment of their sport experience should be our number one priority as parents. Athletics are not a job. Joy and passion should drive the youth sport experience. If your son or daughter wants to play high school sports, earn a scholarship to play in college, or play professionally, they must love their sport. At a certain point, the desire to work the hardest, the willingness to give up things their peers are doing, and the dedication of time and effort to playing their sport will be differentiating factors. If they are not in love with their sport, and they are competing for a spot next to someone who is, they will get left behind.

Parents have a tendency to reduce the level of joy for a young athlete. We focus our attention on the wrong things. "How many hits did you get today?" "How many points did you score today?"

Trust me, I have done this more than once! The problem here is that we focus on results, and results are often outside the athlete's control. Again, if we praise them when they go 4-4, and get upset when they go 0-4, what are we teaching them? We are saying that their ability is based on their results. But results don't tell the entire story. Have they worked hard? Were they a great teammate? Did they respond well when faced with adversity? These are truer tests of their ongoing growth as a young athlete. Results come and go.

Love and passion are driven by aspects of athletics that are within the athlete's control. If they do not feel like they have control of their development, and that their development is based on uncontrollable factors, a "fixed mindset" develops. I can't stress this enough! Focus on *controllable* factors!

When I coached an 11U end-of-the-season "All Star" team, stress levels were at an all-time high. These players were the best of the best in the area, and the expectations of the parents, as well as of the players, were very high. We were very good and everyone knew it. The expectation was that we should win the state tournament.

From the outset it was easy to sense the nerves. The players were very serious and very quiet at practices (definitely not normal for a bunch of eleven-year-olds). When a player made a mistake, he would wear it all over his body. These boys were NOT having fun. They had the weight of the world (or so it seemed to them) on their shoulders. We could not play like this. They were scared, nervous, and tight.

I decided to ask them before our first game if this was "a really big game." To a player, they responded, "Yes, coach, this is a really big game." I then explained to them how much fun they should have in the game, and how they should be great teammates…

cheering for, and supporting one another. I talked to them about how they should walk up to the plate and take "daddy hacks" (one of the players' expressions for high-energy swings). I told them that their hard work had gotten them this far and they should be proud of their accomplishment. I almost immediately saw a change in their body language. Smiles. Energy lifted. More vocal. They were now relaxed and ready to play; they were properly focused on things they could control.

This process turned into a game with our team. Prior to each game, I would ask them, "Another really big game today, right guys?" Before game number two, about half of them were onto me. Half answered, "Yes, coach," while the other half answered, "No, coach." So we would have the discussion again about focusing on things they could control. By the third or fourth game they were all onto me, and were relaxed and ready to play. We didn't lose a game in district play. We didn't lose a game in the state tournament. Best of all, they had fun and played relaxed the entire time.

Communication is the key to unlocking joy. "Did you have fun today?" If the answer is yes, ask them what they enjoyed about it. Steer conversations toward controllables. If they say they had fun because they scored a bunch of points, tell them that's great—it must be because they're sharing the experience with their teammates, bringing great energy, and working hard. If they say they had fun because they love their coaches and their teammates, they are on the right path. If they answer no, ask them why not. If they are not having fun because they are not scoring points, getting hits, etc., steer them toward controllables. Are you working hard? Is your energy good? Are your teammates fun? Are you a good teammate? Generally, if they are not having fun, it is because they are focused on the wrong things: results. They are worried they are not getting enough hits, or scoring enough points. Make sure they know there is so much more to sports than hits and points. Help them focus on controllables.

During your conversations with your son or daughter, ask them how you can best help them enjoy their sport. How can I best support you? How can I help you enjoy your sport? Are you having fun? They may not have clear answers, but they will know that you are in their corner. These questions will let them know that you are focused on their process (enjoying the journey), not the outcomes.

CHAPTER 5

ATHLETIC DEVELOPMENT

"I know that I won't have 'success' (get a hit) every time I step to the plate. I know that I can do everything right and still 'fail.' This puts into perspective how hard the game of baseball is and why I focus on the 'process' over the 'outcome.' I know that my batting average is not a true reflection of how my at-bats have gone."

— Blake Guerin,
University of Iowa, Baseball

Enjoyment in the sport should be the foundation to our approach as parents and coaches. That said, many athletes experience joy through development. The better they get, the better they feel about their efforts and the process. Certainly there is joy in success. So what can we do to provide an environment where optimal athletic development can thrive? It starts with an environment where a "growth mindset" can thrive. Circle back to chapter three and go "all in" on a "growth mindset."

Another major factor in athletic development is intrinsic motivation. Intrinsic motivation is an athlete's ability to be consistently driven by internal forces toward his or her goals. Psychologists Edward L. Deci and Richard M. Ryan, in *Intrinsic*

Motivation and Self-Determination in Human Behavior, have shown that intrinsic motivation provides the best experience, and best performance, in a given task. Deci and Ryan discuss three areas that facilitate, or undermine, intrinsic motivation. If we want to increase intrinsic motivation in our young athlete, we want to focus our attention in these three areas:

- Autonomy
- Competence
- Relatedness

If we want an athlete to be intrinsically motivated, we want to create an environment that steers them toward development of these three traits.

Autonomy

Autonomy is the feeling that I am in control of my destiny. It's the feeling that I am in control of my accomplishments and my failures. If I don't feel like I am in control, and something doesn't go my way, it becomes easy to blame others. If I feel like I am in control, I have earned my successes. I have done the work. I reaped the rewards. If I am in control, and something goes wrong, I take ownership, so I can then begin the process of working to avoid the same mistake.

Autonomy leads to ownership, and ownership is everything. I don't blame others when something goes wrong. I don't point fingers at my teammates or the umpires. If I own it, I can learn and grow from every experience. If I don't own it, how do I learn and grow?

Parents, we must be sure we are giving our young athlete the space to feel a sense of autonomy. If we are constantly pushing, fixing, or dictating, the athlete will never feel a sense of autonomy. Give them room to make mistakes. Give them room to fail. Allow them the space to figure things out on their own. I know this can be tough at times, because we often see an easier path. We see the mistake before it comes. We want to pick them up every time they fall. Fight the urge, and they will be better off in the long run.

I have coached my sons in baseball since they were 5 years old. I know when their energy is good, when their swings are on point, when they're being good teammates, and so on. I have definitely had the impulse to chime in when I see things that I think they should or shouldn't be doing. I fight this urge. It doesn't matter what I see and think. What matters is what they think and feel. When I have loosened the reins, allowing them to explore what works and what doesn't work, I have definitely seen added motivation. They take ownership of their goals, their work ethic, and their process.

Competence

An athlete must feel a certain level of competence in their sport to maintain motivation. If they suck, why would they keep doing it? If they don't feel some sense of competence, they will move on to something else. This is a bit tricky because we generally relate competence to outcomes. If our son or daughter scores a goal (an outcome), they "are competent" in soccer. The young athlete feels this as well. If they get a hit, they "are competent" in baseball. This is why we started giving out participation trophies. If everyone gets a trophy, everyone "is competent" (which feels good), and everyone will continue to want to play. Sadly, as many of you know, this hasn't worked for a variety of reasons (I discuss this more in chapter 10). The question is, how can our son or daughter feel competent without basing their self-assessment of their competence on outcomes? (Not everyone scores a goal or gets a hit every game.) Clearly, we must define competence in a different way. A sense of competence should come from controllable areas. Are they working hard? Are they bouncing back from mistakes? Are they a great teammate? Do they bring consistent high energy to the field?

We can help them by basing our conversations and feedback on controllables. "What are your controllable goals today?" "If you continue to work hard, you will get better." "Your energy was great today!" "You were a great teammate today!" "Your hustle was incredible today!" Athletes will feel a sense of competence in their sport, whether they score a goal or not, if they focus on things they can control.

Competence also comes from recognizing progress. Athletes that feel like they are improving feel more competent, and become more self-driven. "It's not where you start; it's where you finish." Talk to your athlete about areas they are improving. Focus on controllables and tie your comments into "growth mindset" principles. "Your hard work and hustle on the court are leading to better positioning for rebounds." "Your extra batting practice is leading to better and better at-bats." Be genuinely mindful of the progress your son or daughter is making.

One of my clients, a very good 13U soccer player, would become so nervous prior to games that he would ask his coach not to play him. This young player performed amazingly well in practices and in scrimmages, but just prior to games he would become overwhelmed with fear. We began to explore the cause of his fear. He explained that he was afraid to make mistakes. He was afraid he'd turn the ball over, miss a shot, or let a player get around him. He was consumed by fear. As we sat in my office discussing these things, he had tears in his eyes. He certainly didn't want it to be this way, but he didn't know what to do.

When we began discussing what he controlled within each skill (ball handling, shot accuracy, and defense), his mood changed. He is a very driven athlete, and a big part of his drive, as is the case for most top athletes, is the desire to perform well. The problem for him was basing his assessment of his performance on factors outside his control. When we came up with controllable factors that would give him the best chance of success, he began to smile. We broke down each one of his fears. "What do you control that will give you the best chance of handling the ball well?" "Good energy, good footwork, and keeping my eyes up." "What do you control that will give you the best chance of making shots?" "Keeping my head up, having an attack mentality, and staying through the ball when I kick it." "What will give you the best chance of playing great defense?" "Great footwork, great energy, and an attack mentality." He realized that he had control of several things that gave him the best chance of success. He also realized that with focused hard work in those areas, he would continue to get better and better (competence).

I often see competence issues in the 12- to 15-year-old range. Some athletes in this range are simply more advanced than others. Puberty has a huge effect on this. If one kid is simply bigger and stronger than another, he will likely get better results. This leaves the smaller kid feeling less competent. We must be aware of this. If your son or daughter is not as physically mature as their teammates or competition, they will likely be discouraged. But, if they focus on controllables, they can feel a sense of competence no matter their size. If your son or daughter is more physically mature, you should also be aware. Often the more physically mature athlete will get great results. These results can lead to a "fixed" mindset. They are seeing great results and everyone is telling them how good they are. They can come to focus solely on results, which can lead to a reduced focus on things like work ethic, energy, and teamwork. If you have a mature young athlete, keep them dialed into things they can control.

If an athlete is focused on results, feelings of competence will come and go. If an athlete is focused on controllables, feelings of competence will persist.

Relatedness

Relatedness is the feeling that we are supported by and connected to others. Countless studies and plain intuition support the fact that we will be more determined if we are striving toward a common goal with others. Everyone wants to be a part of something bigger than themselves. Determination can skyrocket when we have a sense of relatedness.

Parents, this is why it is so important that we embrace a team-first attitude. We want our young athletes to feel a sense of pride in being a part of something. We want them to feel connected with others. If we constantly talk only about what they are personally doing on the field or in the gym, we are missing this point. Asking a simple question, "How did the team do today?" helps them feel related to their teammates. Even in individual sports, like tennis, golf, or wrestling, a young athlete desires a sense of relatedness. As parents, we can do our best to surround them with athletes that have similar goals and mindsets. Be sure your young athlete feels a sense of relatedness. If he or she does not, things can get very lonely, and their sense of determination can wane.

I have been an assistant high school baseball coach for the last several years. Prior to each season, I sit down with the team to discuss their goals. We talk about outcome goals, why the goals are important, and how we will achieve the goals. It is important to establish these goals early on, decide why they are important, and create a plan for how we will go about achieving them.

One of the biggest things to come out of this goal-setting process is establishing ways we will create relatedness within the program. When we start discussing how we will achieve our goals, there is invariably a component of team, teamwork, support, etc., that comes up. Here is an example:

> **Goal**: Win the conference.
>
> **Why**? Having this goal will push us every day in practice, keep our focus high in games, and challenge us to be the best we can be.
>
> **How**? We have to bring our best to every practice. We have to support and challenge each other at all times.

Bingo!! "Support and challenge each other"—that's relatedness! There is always a relatedness component to the "how" question. This is how we create relatedness within our team.

CHAPTER 6

PERSONAL DEVELOPMENT

"Don't root your whole identity in your sport."
— *Lucie Henrich,*
Gustavus Adolphus College, Soccer

What do you hope your son or daughter gets out of their sports experience?

There is no bigger question to ask yourself, and it is well worth taking some time to think about. Ten, twenty, or thirty years from now, what do you hope your son or daughter will have gained from participating in their sport? We get wrapped up in this season, this game, or this at-bat. Why does it matter? I look back at games over the years that I thought at the time were "big games." Reflecting now, I can't even remember exactly which games were the "big games." I do recall the Little League State Finals, and I do recall feeling like *that* was a "big game." We won that game. That was fun. But what if we had lost? Would the lives of the kids have turned out differently? No, their lives would not be any different. In retrospect, I actually think they could have possibly learned more if we had lost. It's truly about the journey. Time we spent together. Lessons we learned.

We say that sports build character, but do they? For me, the building of character is not automatic; to build character, we must intentionally focus on building the character skills that we desire. If we lose, and we react poorly, are we building a quality character skill? If we strike out, and throw our bat, are we building a quality character skill? Before I go further, let me define why I use the term "character skill" vs. "character trait."

Generally, people talk about "character traits." The term "trait" generally is thought to be something people are born with. I prefer the term "character skill," because a skill is something that can be acquired. Semantics yes, but words matter. When I talk with young athletes about acquiring a skill, they immediately think it is something they can work toward. I believe people can achieve changes in their character, so I use the term character skill.

So what do you hope your son or daughter gets out of their sports experience? Let's take a look at several character skills that can be nurtured through the sports experience and some ways we can nurture these skills.

- Hard Work
- Competitiveness
- Focus
- Resilience
- Confidence
- Selflessness
- Respect
- Appreciativeness
- Humility
- Accountability

Which of these skills do you hope your son or daughter builds through sports? Are there others? As you look through this list, ask yourself, "If my young athlete acquires these skills through his or her sport, what else is there to gain?" If your son or daughter learns the importance of hard work, becomes more resilient, is disciplined, is respectful, and is honest, what else is there? Don't you think he or she will have great success both on and off the field?

When I work with young athletes, I emphasize the development of these skills. This development is within their control. This development will maximize their abilities both on and off the field. What character skills do you value? Go through the list above with your athlete. Write down which skills your young athlete will work to acquire. Focus on the development of those skills and let the rest fall to the wayside.

Let's go through each of the skills listed above to give you ideas of how you can nurture these skills.

Hard Work

The character skill of hard work originates from a strong desire to succeed. I'll only work really hard at something if I am passionate about whatever goal I am striving for. The foundation is then built from having goals, having a strong "why" related to those goals, and creating a process for achieving those goals. Here is the process for creating the foundation:

1. Talk with your son or daughter about their goals. Write down their goals: short-term (3 months or less), mid-term (3 months to a year), and long-term (more than a year).
2. Once you have established the goals, ask your athlete "why" each of these goals are important to them. What

inspires them to reach for these goals? What will they have accomplished when they reach these goals? Goals are important, no doubt, but passion is driven by the "why." Dedication is driven by the "why."

3. Discuss and write down "how" (the process) they will achieve their goals. What things must they do to reach their goals?

4. Discuss and write down "why" each of these process items are important to them. How will they feel if they work hard at each of these process items? How will they be different if they work hard at each of these process items?

Four Steps:

1. **Goal.**
2. **Why?**
3. **How?**
4. **Why?**

Be sure the athlete is writing down controllable factors when it comes to their "how." The goal may not always be within their control, but the "how" should be. The "how" becomes their focus, and the goal, or the end result, becomes a by-product of how well they do with their "how." This becomes a self-driven process (revisit the Chapter 5 discussion on the self-determination theory). They set a goal. They believe strongly in the purpose for achieving that goal. They set up a process that will help them reach the goal. If they reach the goal, the process is a good one. If they don't reach the goal, they must rethink the process, or how they followed the process. A by-product of this type of goal setting is a growth mindset. "I didn't reach my goal; now what can I change or do better to reach it?" Super powerful stuff!

Let's be clear: a 10-year-old athlete may not be as strong at goal setting, describing their "why," and putting together a "how" as a 17-year-old. However, discussing these elements and thinking about them can be done at a very young age.

A helpful tip when creating the "why" for many athletes is to have them think about how they will feel once they have accomplished their goal. An example: Their goal is to average 15 points per game. They can then think about how they will feel about themselves if by the end of the season they have averaged 15 points per game.

Here is an example of what the goal setting process might look like:

> **Goal**: Bat .400 this season
>
> **Why?** This goal is important to me because batting .400 will put me on base a lot. Being on base a lot will give our team a better chance to score runs, which gives us a better chance to win more games. I will also feel proud of this accomplishment and the work that I put in to achieve it.
>
> **How?** I will hit 6 days per week between now and the start of the season. I will spend at least half my time hitting balls to the opposite field because I know that is something I need to work on.
>
> **Why?** It will teach me the importance of hard work and dedication. It will also help build my confidence as I go into the season.

Throughout their years in sport, and when switching from one sport to another, this goal setting process should be done. If you notice the desire to work hard is waning in your son or daughter, go through this process.

A second huge piece in developing the skill of hard work are the principles of intrinsic motivation (Autonomy, Competence, and Relatedness) that were discussed in chapter 5. Revisit those principles as well.

I assume we would all like our sons or daughters to understand the idea that hard work is the way to success, not just on the field, but off it. Sadly, much of the information young people are receiving these days sends a different message. Social media tends to create the appearance that success is easy. Young people must believe that work (the process) will affect their outcome. As parents, we must emphasize the effort over the outcome. We should always center feedback to our children around their effort. It should not be, "You were great today; those 3 hits were amazing." It should instead be, "You've worked really hard; you should be proud of yourself."

Competitive

The most important thing in developing a competitive athlete is understanding and defining what it means to be competitive. There is a lot of confusion with both parents and athletes about what it means to be a great competitor. I often hear parents and coaches telling their athletes to "compete." When I speak to athletes about this, they are often confused about what thoughts and actions equate to being a great competitor. Athletes need to understand what controllable factors they must work toward to become a better competitor. Here is a list of controllable factors for becoming a great competitor:

- Great energy
- Great attitude
- Great effort
- Confidence
- Accountability (for mistakes)

- Resilient (bouncing back after a mistake)
- Great teammate

These are controllables. They are not always easy to control, and are certainly skills that need to be developed, but they are within the athlete's control. A great competitor does not let the scoreboard dictate any of the controllables on the list. Each one of these skills is a character skill that is discussed in this book. Development of great character skills will make the athlete a great competitor. Again, define these skills for your athlete. Discuss when and why each skill is needed.

Competitiveness is controllable. Express and support the controllable aspects of being a great competitor: energy, attitude, effort, confidence, accountability, resilience, and teamwork.

Focused

Like competitiveness, the term "focused" is not always relatable for an athlete. They know they should be focused, but they do not necessarily know the actionable steps to be or stay focused. The ability to focus is the art of being *present*. Not thinking about the past or looking into the future. *This* pitch. *This* play. What is my responsibility on this pitch?

A lack of focus is simply a wandering mind. Having focus is being clear-minded about what is directly in front of us. The art of being present is NOT easy. Adults go on week-long meditation retreats to work on being present. Distractions are everywhere. Young people these days have it way harder than we did: social media, phones in their pockets, and on and on. We must teach them how to be more focused—more present.

I'd like to discuss two areas I think young people can work on to become more focused. The first is long-term focus. An example of long-term focus is goal setting. The second is short-term focus.

This type of focus would be focusing on one game, one at-bat, or one pitch.

Long-Term Focus

Getting a young athlete to focus day to day on long term goals can be tough. There are ups and downs. There are days where the effort and energy are great, and days where they are not so good. To foster a more consistent level of effort and energy, develop the skill of goal setting. Take a look back at the "Hard Working" character skill from this chapter to revisit goal setting. Here is a quick recap of goal setting from that section:

1. Set goals and write them down.
2. Talk about and write down the "why" associated with each goal.
3. Talk about and write down the "how" (the process) for achieving each goal.
4. Talk about and write down "why" each of these process items are important.

Setting goals in this manner gives goals meaning and fuels the athletes' purpose for achieving their goals. Meaning and purpose drive effort and energy. If your son or daughter wakes up each morning and is driven by meaning and purpose, they will consistently chase their goals.

Short-Term Focus

The first step in ensuring short-term focus is giving the athlete specific things on which to focus. If they don't have a specific focus, their minds will wander. We do this by giving them routines. Routines are mental cues and physical actions that they repeat over and over. Routines create a focus—an intent. Routines bring the mind and body into the present moment.

The physical (body) portions of routines are done in all sports and by every athlete. There are pre-game routines (warm-ups, pre-game catch, etc.) and in-game routines (on-deck circle, just prior to entering a game, etc.). These are routines that focus on getting the body ready for action. The mind, or more specifically what thoughts we are having, is not generally considered within these routines, but definitely needs to be. We want the athlete to add specific thoughts into their routines. The proper thoughts can help bring them into the present moment and aid in short-term focus. Our thoughts trigger our action, so athletes should be preparing both their minds and bodies for action.

Here are examples of routines that can help the athlete be focused and in the present moment:

Routine 1 (pre-game warm-ups/baseball):
- During dynamic warm-ups (movement-based warm-up) the athlete says to himself, "It's going to be a great day."
- During pre-game catch the athlete says to himself, "My throws will be on point all day."
- During pre-game batting practice the athlete says to himself, "Great at-bats, all day."

Routine 2 (in-game/softball):
- The shortstop takes a deep breath as the pitcher is taking the sign from the catcher (breathing calms the mind and body).
- The shortstop steps forward, right foot, left foot, as the pitcher winds up (preparing the body).
- The shortstop thinks, "Hit this ball to me!" as the pitcher releases the ball (this "final thought" focuses the mind).

Routine 3 (in-game/basketball):

- A basketball player is fouled and is stepping to the free-throw line.
- She steps to the line, right foot, left foot (physical readiness).
- She receives the ball from the referee.
- She takes a deep breath and stares at the basket (calming the mind and body).
- She dribbles 3 times (physical readiness and slowing her mind).
- She thinks to herself, "Nothing but net" ("final thought" to focus the mind).

Routines give the athlete something to focus on (to be present-minded). As they build routines, they can then become aware of times when their mind is wandering. This awareness is the first step. The second step is the ability to refocus when the mind wanders. This is extremely important because the mind will wander. Remember, your athlete will not be able to refocus unless they know what they should be focusing on in the first place. They must build similar physical and mental routines to those discussed above so they know where to place their focus! Once those routines are built, they can use the following method to get refocused when their mind wanders. This method is called the "3 R's." The 3 R's are: Recognize, Release, and Re-Focus. Here is how it works:

Recognize

When a young athlete is struggling to stay present and focus on the task at hand, they must first Recognize that they are distracted. The mind easily and unconsciously changes course.

As I said earlier, this is even an issue for adults, so expecting young people to continuously remain present is an unfair expectation. So how can young people recognize when they are losing focus if it happens unconsciously? Again, they must first understand what they should be focused on. Developing awareness of when they are NOT focused on their routines then must become a part of their practice. After practices and games, they can ask themselves, "How did I do with my routines today? Was I able to stay focused?" The more they become aware of times they are pulled away from their routines (the present moment), the more they can start to bring themselves back to the present. With younger athletes (generally twelve and under), this is something you as the parent can help them with. "It seems you sometimes lose focus when a player on your team makes a mistake." This can help them become aware of situations that take them out of their routines. If they are aware of these situations, they can be better prepared the next time a similar situation arises. The tenets of meditation teach us that we will inevitably lose focus, so that key skill is being able to bring ourselves back to focus when our mind wanders. The same holds true in athletics. The sooner the athlete can become aware of when he or she is pulled off course, the more quickly they can get themselves back on track. Here is an example of the ability to recognize distracting thoughts:

A batter takes strike one. His thoughts become wrapped up in his dislike for the call. "Dang, that was way outside. Now I'm down 0-1. This umpire sucks." These are distracted thoughts that will not help the player to achieve his best possible outcome in this at-bat. He must recognize this as unhelpful thinking. He has a routine that he uses between pitches, but he can't focus on his routine. He is distracted by his thoughts about the stinky umpire. Since he knows his routine, and he has practiced his routine, he is able to recognize that he cannot access it. Since he has recognized his inability to be present in his routine, he can go to the second "R."

Relax

Relaxing is simply taking a few seconds, once he has recognized that he is distracted, to pull himself back to the present moment. Here the athlete simply takes a deep breath: four seconds in, four seconds out. Breathing is amazing; controlled breathing calms the mind and the body.

Generally, an athlete will lose focus because something happens that heightens physical and mental anxiety. Consider the baseball batter example above. The tough call raises his anxiety and initiates a flow of unwanted thoughts. When those thoughts creep in, remaining present seems impossible. However, a deep breath can give the athlete a sense of physical and mental calm, and the time needed to regain useful thoughts.

The wide benefits of controlled breathing should not be underestimated. When the athlete loses focus, breathe. When they are feeling anxious, breathe. When they are feeling overly excited, breathe. This takes some practice. When we tell an athlete that hasn't practiced breathing to "breathe," they take a hurried breath that helps nothing. Sometimes these hurried breaths can cause even more anxiety! Once the athlete has taken a little time to slow things down, they can now re-focus.

Re-Focus

Re-focusing means getting back to the routine that they have practiced. The following is an example of what a shortstop using the 3 R's might look like:

A ball goes through his legs. "Dang it, I should have had that one. I stink today. I just let my team down."

- Recognize : these thoughts aren't a part of his routine.
- Relax: he slows things down with a deep breath.
- Refocus: he gets back to his routine.

He takes one more deep breath while the pitcher is getting signs from the catcher. When the pitcher is winding up, he steps forward, right foot, left foot, and thinks to himself, "Hit this ball to me."

The ability to properly focus relies both on the knowledge of what to focus on and how to refocus when the mind wanders. Talk with your son or daughter about areas in which they seem to lack focus. Be sure they know what they should be focused on and why. Lastly, discuss with them ways that they can return to focus when their mind wanders.

Long-term focus will improve as your son or daughter masters the art of goal setting. A focused athlete has goals, a "why" driving their goals, and a "how" for achieving their goals.

Short-term focus will improve as your son or daughter masters their routines. Routines bring the mind and body into the present moment.

Resilient

Resilience is the ability to learn and grow from mistakes and failures. Kids must fail in order to build resilience. As parents, we must allow our kids to fail. How can they learn to recover from their failures if they are constantly sheltered from things that may cause them to fail? I am not talking about abandoning them completely...but all too often, we shelter them from failure. We must understand that failure is a great teacher. Failure is a sign that an adjustment needs to be made. If my son strikes out, what can he do to get better? Mistakes and failure are simply an opportunity to learn and grow. This circles us back yet again to a "growth mindset." Mistakes and failures do not define a young person who has a "growth mindset." They are simply signs that improvement is needed.

We must also be sure that our sons and daughters learn to take ownership of their mistakes and failures. If they blame others, they lose the opportunity to learn and grow. If my son blames the umpire when he strikes out, he loses any opportunity to learn from his at-bat. If a teammate makes an error on the last play of a game, and my son blames the teammate for the loss, my son gives up an opportunity to consider what he could have done differently in the game.

I think a lack of resilience is a big problem with today's young athletes for the two reasons listed above. We shelter them from mistakes and failure, and we allow them to blame others when they do make a mistake or fail. We must give them the space to fail. We must stress the need for them to own their mistakes and failures. We must then convey to them the importance of learning and growing from their mistakes and failures. Stress to them that everyone makes mistakes, but not everyone learns from their mistakes.

Resilience is built around falling down and getting up. As parents, we must not shelter our young athletes from potential failures. We must give them the space to fail, and support them as they work through processes to overcome their failures. They must own their mistakes. Ownership gives them an opportunity to learn and grow.

Confident

There are several ways to build confidence. However, none are more effective than putting in the work. When your son or daughter steps to the free throw line, steps in the batter's box, or gets on the mound, they know deep down whether or not they have worked hard. Look back at the "hard working" section. If they have done the work, they will be more confident.

Building confidence also circles us back to the importance of a "growth mindset." I make a mistake, I learn from the mistake, I put in the work to get better, I get better. Repeat. Then I make fewer and fewer mistakes, and confidence builds.

Often the lack of confidence in sports is directly attached to a desired outcome. If the outcome is not something I believe I can succeed at, I lose confidence. What we choose as the desired outcome in sports is frequently outside of our control, and if we can't control the outcome, we lose confidence. Take for example the desired outcome of an at-bat. The desired outcome for most players is getting a hit. But do we control whether or not we get a hit? We do not. How then can we be ultimately confident that we will get a hit? We cannot then base our level of confidence on the knowledge that we will get a hit. Sadly, sports are filled with many uncontrollable outcomes that athletes strive for. The goal is to win the game. Do we control whether or not we win? We do not. The goal is to score 20 points tonight. Do we control whether or not we will get 20 points? We do not. So, to walk to the plate with confidence, we must teach our young athletes to focus on things within their control. They control their thoughts and actions. They control the thoughts they have while walking to the plate, and their thoughts at the plate. They control whether or not they take full energy swings. They control their response to adversity. They control their energy and attitude. Here is a list of things that an athlete does not control. Read this list carefully and ask yourself if you or your athlete tries to control any of these things:

- How many hits they get
- How many points they score
- How many touchdowns they score

- How many passes they complete
- How many yards they rush for
- How many goals they score
- How many assists they get
- How many strikeouts they get
- How many hits they give up
- Whether they win or lose

Here is a list of things they do control, and by properly controlling them, they will have the best chance of success:

- Their thoughts
- Their energy
- Their attitude
- Their effort
- Being a great teammate
- Their preparation
- Their response to adversity
- Their work ethic

These lists aren't exhaustive, but you get the idea. If we can help our young athletes to focus on the things they do control, they will be more confident. They will know that they control their ability to be successful within those things. Can you walk to the plate with good and useful thoughts in your head? Yes I can. Can you hustle up and down the court, playing with great energy? Yes I can.

I realize the ultimate goal is to win games, get hits, score goals, etc. But if we can focus our young athlete on the controllable skills that give them the best chance of successfully reaching these outcome goals (winning games, getting hits, scoring goals, etc.), they will have more confidence.

We must speak to young athletes about the process that will give them the best chance of success. Are they doing everything they can to prepare (working hard in practice)? Are they walking to the plate with useful thoughts? Are they taking their best swings at the plate? If they are doing these things, they are giving themselves the best chance of success, and they will gain confidence. This is where confidence comes from: *a belief that I control my outcome.* But again, if I don't control my desired outcome, I will not be confident.

Confidence is all about controllables. I am confident when I believe I can achieve a desired outcome. We must help our athletes to establish what is and what is not within their control.

Selfless

The character skill of selflessness is another game changer for young athletes. I think it is pretty obvious how an athlete that embodies selflessness can benefit teammates, but I'll touch on it a bit anyway. A selfless teammate is constantly lifting up others. A selfless teammate holds others accountable. A selfless teammate wants success for their teammates. A selfless teammate always puts the team first. It is easy to see how a selfless teammate can benefit those around them.

There is also a personal benefit from being selfless. Selflessness is reciprocated. Teammates will root for their selfless teammate. Teammates will support their selfless teammate. Coaches love coaching selfless players. The selfless player will also play more relaxed and with more confidence. They have the support of their coaches and teammates. Since they put "we" over "me," they are not so wrapped up in personal outcomes. The selfless teammate knows their worth on the team is way bigger than how many hits they get or how many points they score.

You can help your athlete to become more selfless by asking them questions about the team. "How did the team do today?" Ask them questions about specific players on the team. At games, cheer for everyone. Steer clear of personalized questions like, "How many hits did you get today?" If your son or daughter chooses to reflect on personal statistics, steer them toward a discussion about the team.

A selfless athlete has more fun, plays with more confidence, and has better support in their development. We must emphasize "we" over "me."

Respectful

Athletes that respect their teammates, their opponents, their coaches, and the referees will have a greater athletic experience than athletes that do not.

Treating teammates with respect will be reciprocated. Treating teammates with a lack of respect will also be reciprocated. We want our athletes to support their teammates and have the support of their teammates. This support system creates a better sport experience for the athlete. They have more fun, play more relaxed, and garner more support in their development from teammates and coaches.

Respecting opponents is a true sign of character. It is generally pretty easy for an athlete to respect those closest to them. It is tougher to respect athletes they are competing against, but they should take on this challenge. An athlete with a "growth mindset" wants the other team's best performance to challenge them. They don't want to create an environment where their opponent is distracted by disrespectful actions. Respect once again will be reciprocated, bringing out the best in both teams.

"Coach doesn't like me." "Coach plays favorites." "Coach doesn't know what he's doing." Disrespect toward coaches generally stems from a lack of ownership. We want our young athletes to take ownership of their personal process—the good and the bad. Directing disapproval at coaches dissociates athletes from their process. When our athletes place blame on their coaches, they lose any chance to learn and grow from the experience.

Our athletes do not control referees, and we always want the athlete to focus on what they control. If the athlete chooses to disrespect the referee, they are giving control to the referee. As parents, we must not disrespect referees. If we disrespect the referee, we are telling our young athlete that the referee is in control. Control what you can control!

Respect should be given at all times to everyone involved. It is our duty as parents to lead by example. We must speak highly of our son or daughter's teammates. We must show respect to the opponents and their fans. We must support coaches, even if we don't agree with all of their coaching techniques. We must treat referees with respect, even when we don't agree with their call.

Appreciative

When our young athlete appreciates their sport, and everything and everyone that comes with it, they are more passionate about the sport. If they appreciate their coaches, their coaches will love to be a part of their development. If they appreciate their teammates, their teammates will want to be a part of their experience. If they appreciate playing their sport, they will be more committed to it. If they appreciate the referees, the referees will enjoy their experience more, which can undoubtedly make the experience better for everyone. If they appreciate what we are doing for them, and giving them, we will be excited to play any role we can in their sports experience.

If our young athletes do not show appreciation, they will lose the support of their teammates and coaches, and undoubtedly we will have a harder time supporting their journey.

We must once again lead by example when it comes to appreciation. We must be sure to show thanks to supportive teammates, coaches, and other parents. We must also hold our athletes accountable to showing appreciation for those around them. Ask them if they remembered to thank their coaches after their practice. Ask them to thank the referees after the game. If our athletes learn to show appreciation, even for the little things, it will certainly heighten their overall athletic experience.

Humble

A humble athlete is a confident athlete. There is no need for a confident athlete to outwardly express their ego. They believe in themselves, in their process, and in their character. Who they are on the field does not need to be highlighted.

If your athlete is struggling with humility, they undoubtedly have a lack of confidence. They try to improve their self-worth by verbalizing or acting a certain way, a way that they feel will earn them respect from within, and from others.

Re-visit the section on confidence (page 40). Again, a confident athlete is a humble athlete. They trust who they are, both as a person and an athlete. A large part of humility comes from their self-worth off the field. If they have strong values and focus on the type of person they hope to become (character skills), they will act with humility.

For our athletes to compete with humility, we must focus on character development. Who they are is *way* more important than how they perform.

Encouraging

This is a trait of a great teammate. An encouraging teammate lifts up the people around them. An encouraging teammate is a fountain, not a drain. Yes, this is a character skill that can be developed. An encouraging teammate reaps the rewards from being a great teammate. They are supported by their teammates and coaches. By encouraging others, they reduce the stress of the sport, putting the skill of encouragement before thoughts of personal performance. An encouraging teammate will develop faster, play more relaxed, and have a better sports experience.

As parents, we should simply ask our athletes to encourage others. They will see the benefits immediately, garnering the support of teammates and coaches. Ask them to lift others up. Help them encourage a teammate who is feeling down. We should model this behavior. We should be encouraging to our son or daughter, their teammates, the opponent, and the coaches.

Accountable

Athletes that are accountable (take ownership) for their successes, failures, ups, downs, wins, and losses have the best chance of consistent growth. This goes back to the "growth mindset" principles. If we give up ownership in any situation, we lose the opportunity to learn and grow from that situation.

I see a lack of ownership often with athletes. This can often stem from the desire to protect their ego. They have been told that they should be confident, act confident, and perform with confidence. This can cause an athlete to fake confidence. They make a mistake, but don't want to admit the mistake because it might show weakness. Admitting weakness translates, for many athletes, to a lack of confidence. "I made a mistake, but if I admit that mistake, I don't look confident." This makes sense. If they associate mistakes with weakness, they lose confidence if they admit their mistake. So the athlete decides they are better off placing blame elsewhere, and they don't have to admit the mistake. This is fake confidence. Deep down they know they made the mistake. If their confidence is then based on never making mistakes, they will constantly be searching for confidence. Mistakes are inevitable.

Young people are also surrounded by social media sites that show all the greatness in the world. The millionaires, the sweet cars, the amazing houses, etc. They assume the millionaire athletes never struggle, because they don't show their struggles on Instagram. They never see the mistakes, the failures, or the pain that is a part of life.

We must make sure our sons and daughters understand that mistakes and failures are a part of growth. We must make sure they know that mistakes and failures are not an attack on who they are as a person. We must make sure they know that how they respond to their mistakes and failures is what is important. We must make sure they know that their confidence should not be tied to mistakes and failures. They should be taught that confidence is at its highest when they can admit their mistakes and failures. A truly confident person has the strength to admit their weaknesses.

CHAPTER 7

JOURNALING

"Control the controllables. Don't let something you can't control impact how you compete."

— Keenan Mork,
University of Notre Dame, Baseball

Journaling is an amazing mental performance tool to aid in the personal and physical development of a young athlete. Journaling helps them consistently focus on their goals, their why, and their how. It leads them toward development of their physical, mental, and character skills. It helps focus their minds on controllables. It aids in the elimination of distractions. It aids in all aspects of their sports experience. And, as a side benefit, it also aids the parent experience!

When my son Will was in 8th grade, he wrestled with the high school team. He started the season 0-10. He was getting beaten pretty badly in most matches, either getting pinned or losing by a wide point margin. Prior to every match, Will would journal. He would write down the physical skills he would work on during the match—things like a single-leg takedown or a wrist roll. He would write down mental skills he would work on, like responding well when adversity hit. Lastly, he would write down the character skills he would focus on, things like great energy or humility. Following each match, Will journaled again. He wrote down the things he did well and the things he needed to work on. If he didn't know what he needed to work on, he would ask his coaches. Every day after a match he would show up at practice knowing what he needed to work on. The coaches were eager to help because they knew he was invested in getting better. Slowly but surely, Will started to narrow the gap with his opponents. Around the middle of the season, things began to turn around. Will finished the season with a 12-12 record. That might not look great at first glance, but he went 12-2 in his final 14 matches. His biggest win came toward the end of the season when he beat a kid that had pinned him early in the season.

Journaling undoubtedly played a huge role in Will's turnaround. It would have been easy for him to get discouraged in the early part of the season, but journaling helped him to focus on consistent growth. Journaling prior to matches gave him controllable things to focus on that he knew would make him a better wrestler. Journaling after matches allowed him to focus on positive things he had done each match. Journaling allowed him to focus on development, while outcomes, the wins and losses, became secondary. Journaling inspired added support from his coaches. Journaling after his matches also provided an end point to his wrestling for the day. He would journal and move on with no need to mentally replay his matches any further. This isn't to say by any means that Will was never upset after a loss. He was. But it didn't linger, and he kept striving to get better every day.

Here is how journaling works.

Step 1: Goal setting

Discuss goals, the "why," and the "how" (the process), and have your athlete write them in their journal.

Remember, goals can be short and/or long term. For younger athletes, it may just be goals for the season. For older athletes, it may be goals for the season, the year, the next five years, and maybe even longer. Whatever the case, for each goal they should have the "why" and the "how."

Some athletes are driven more by *outcome* goals—things like batting average, points scored, etc. These types of goals are fine, but they must have a process ("how") for achieving these goals. They should also include *controllable* goals, and among those should be physical, mental, and character goals.

Example:

Outcome Goal
Goal: *To hit .400.*

Why? *It will help my team and is a good measure of what I think I can hit.*

How (the process)? *Practice every day. Walk to the plate with confidence. Have a plan when I get to the plate.* (Remember that the "how" must be things that are 100% controllable.)

Controllable Goals
Goal: *Become better at hitting balls to the opposite field* (physical goal).

Why? *It will allow me to hit more pitches, which will make me a better hitter.*

How? *Work on hitting balls to the opposite field every day in practice.*

Goal: *To compete with more confidence* (mental goal).

Why? *It will allow me to be the best player I can be.*

How? *By focusing on my controllable goals, not the outcome.*

Goal: *Become a better teammate* (character goal).

Why? *I know it will be good for the team and I want to get to know my teammates better.*

How? *Be more encouraging. Show up with a good attitude every day.*

I think it is easy to see how powerful this type of goal setting can be. This also becomes a guide to their development for the season. It becomes a reference, during times of success or struggle, to keep them headed in the right direction. Athletes can often get wrapped up in one at-bat, or one game. Journaling can help them navigate the ups and downs because they will always be keeping the end in mind.

I have had athletes that wanted to write down their outcome goals, like batting average or points scored. They felt like writing down these goals would help push them toward success. In many of these cases, the athlete ended up focusing too much on the outcome. This outcome-based focus then led to pressure to perform, and reduced focus on consistent development and having a great experience.

An example of this would be a baseball player that has an outcome goal of hitting .400 for the season. Let's say this player starts the season going 0-10. Now he starts to press. "I have to get a hit this at-bat." This added pressure causes anxiety and draws him away from his controllables and his process. Again, if your athlete sets some outcome-based goals, be sure they are focused on the process.

Step 2: Journaling before and after practices

Before Practice:

Prior to practice, the athlete should write down their goals for the practice. These goals should include at least one physical-related goal ("I will get better at free throws today"), one mental goal ("I will shake it off quickly if I make a mistake"), and one character-related goal ("I will be a great teammate today"). Notice I use the word "will" in these sentences. These are controllable actions, so the word "will" brings life to their actions. The athlete should then write down "how" they will go about accomplishing these goals. This system begins to create a process of goal attainment and an accountability toward reaching their goals. It also focuses their attention not only on physical skills, but also on mental and character skills. At younger ages, writing down one or two goals and how they will achieve those goals is great. Older athletes may have multiple areas of focus.

Pre-practice goal setting example:

Goal (physical): *Today I will get better at hitting the ball to the opposite field.*

How? *In my batting practice I will attempt to hit every ball to the opposite field.*

Goal (mental): *Today I will take every repetition with confidence.*

How? *Prior to each repetition, I will say to myself, "I've got this."*

Goal (character): *Today I will be the hardest worker on the field.*

How? *I will hustle everywhere I go. I will be the first one taking repetitions and the last one done.*

After practice:

Following practice, the athlete should summarize how they performed. There are three things to cover here:

1. What went well?
2. What do I want to improve?
3. How will I work on the things I want to improve?

After-practice example:

Goal (physical):
What went well? *I had great energy and great focus today in my work to get better at hitting balls to the opposite field.*

What do I want to improve? *I still need to work on hitting the ball to the opposite field.*

How will I get better at hitting the ball to the opposite field? *I need to remind myself to hit the ball deeper when I'm working on it.*

Goal (mental)
What went well? *I took most of my repetitions with confidence and it felt great.*

What do I want to improve? *When I miss-hit a few balls, I get frustrated quickly.*

How will I get better at not becoming frustrated quickly? *I will focus on growth, not outcome.*

Goal (character):
What went well? *I mostly did great on recovering when something bad happened. When that one ball went through my legs, I let it go, and re-focused immediately.*

What do I want to improve? *I still struggled at times to recover.*

How will I get better at recovering faster? I will continue to work on recognizing when I am having negative thoughts and think to myself, "Next pitch."

This after-practice goal summarizing then sets the stage for their next practice. At the next practice, they can look back at their summary from this practice and identify things they want to work on. This becomes a consistent mechanism for progress.

Step 3: Journaling before and after games

Journaling before games:

Journaling before games is slightly different than before practices. Before games, we want the athlete to write down their goals and then write down the "how" (the process) that will give them the *best chance* for reaching those goals. Remember that the process should be 100% within their control. Be sure they include physical goals, mental goals, and character goals.

Example:

Goal (physical): *I will score at least 12 points.*

How? *Hustle up and down the court. Move without the ball. Take the ball to the rim.*

Goal (mental): *I will take every shot with confidence.*

How? *I will constantly be thinking, "I've got this."*

Goal (character): *Be a great teammate and leader.*

How? *I will be very vocal on both ends of the court.*

As I said earlier, I have worked with several athletes that like to set goals that are outside of their control, like how many points they score. If this is the case with your athlete, have them set goals that are only 100% within their control.

Example:

Goal (physical): *I will be more focused on scoring points today.*

How? *I will hustle up and down the court, move without the ball, and take open shots when I get them.*

Goal (mental): *I will take every shot with confidence.*

How? *I will constantly be thinking, "I've got this."*

Goal (character): *I will be a great teammate and leader.*

How? *I will be very vocal on both ends of the court.*

Journaling after games:

Similar to after practice, this is just a summary of how the game went. They should look specifically at their goals for the game, consider whether those goals were met, assess things that went well, and what they want to work on moving forward.

Example:

Goal (physical):

What went well? *I did a great job of moving without the ball.*

What do I want to work on? *I need to continue to work on taking my shot when I am open.*

How will I work on taking my shot when I'm open? *In practice, I will work hard to recognize good and bad times to take my shot.*

Goal (mental):

What went well? *I took almost every shot with confidence.*

What do I want to work on? *Taking every shot with confidence.*

How will I work on taking every shot with confidence? *When I miss a shot, I need to let it go and think, "I'll get the next one."*

Goal (character):

What went well? *I was a great teammate and leader today.*

What do I want to work on? *When I missed a couple of shots, my energy went down, and I started to have some negative thoughts.*

How will I be a great teammate and leader no matter what? *I will always put the team first.*

Journaling is so powerful. It creates a growth mindset. It increases confidence by focusing on controllables. It enhances self-determination by giving the athlete the power in their development. It focuses them not only on performance, but on mental and character development as well.

The Parental Benefit

One of the biggest concerns I hear from both parents and young athletes is regarding what a parent should or should not be communicating to the athlete. How hard should I push? What should I say during the ride to the game? What should I say after the game? Journaling guides these conversations and makes them much easier and more valuable for both the parent and the athlete.

Discussions prior to the game should be based around goals for the game. What performance, mental, and character goals does the athlete have for the game? What controllable factors will they focus on to attain those goals? After the game, the athlete should journal how they did in relation to their goals and write what they want to work on moving forward. We can then ask them to share their thoughts. We will then be able to have constructive conversations.

Journaling has been a game changer for me and my sons. Pre-game conversations prior to journaling were generally all over the place and would often end up steering my sons toward uncontrollable goals, such as, "How many hits will you get today?" These conversations would certainly not be focused on the "how." They would have little or nothing to do with mental or character development. Post-game conversations were more of the same. "You played great" followed a game where they had 3 or 4 hits. "You didn't play your best" followed games where they didn't get many hits.

When they started journaling, pre-game conversations became based on controllables, physical development, mental development, and character development. Post-game conversations became based on reflection of successes and ongoing development.

I can't recommend journaling enough. Journaling can change the game for your athlete. It can also change the game for you and even change your relationship with your son or daughter.

CHAPTER 8

AGE-SPECIFIC CONSIDERATIONS

"The mental part of the game is the biggest challenge. I'm glad I started taking the mental game seriously at a young age."

— Blake Guerin,
University of Iowa, Baseball

The following age group considerations should be considered a guide. Timing of physical and personal development, as well as other characteristics, can certainly vary from one athlete to the next. Before jumping into these, let me say that the most important thing with any of the age groups is communication. What are your son's or daughter's goals? Why are these goals important to them? Are these goals within their control? How will they go about achieving these goals? How can you best support these goals? What do they want and what do they need from you? Have these conversations frequently.

Age 7-9

When my oldest son, Will, was seven, he began playing "coach pitch" baseball. Coach pitch is when the coach throws the pitches to the hitter instead of players throwing to each other.

This would be Will's first experience with organized sport. He had played some tee ball and soccer, but those were more about rolling the ball out and making sure no one got hurt. As I recall, the first day of practice consisted of the kids meeting each other, the coaches introducing themselves, and the coaches asking if any other parents wanted to help out. I decided to give coaching a shot. It was so much fun. Will is now twenty one years old, and several of his current best friends were introduced to him on that first day of practice.

In retrospect, I consider both Will and myself very lucky to have ended up with that group of coaches, players, and families. Everyone involved considered winning important and one of the goals, but winning was regarded as an end result of doing the little things right. We taught the players the importance of being on time. We taught them how to be good teammates. We taught them the value of hard work. We taught them to be respectful to coaches, umpires, and their opponents. The parents were awesome. They were supportive of not just their own sons, but of all the players on the team.

Around this same time, when Will was in first grade, he started getting into trouble at school. Pretty much once a week (at least it felt that often) my wife and I would receive a call from the vice-principal at his elementary school. Generally, his offense was some type of aggressiveness on the playground. My wife and I began looking into approaches that might help guide Will toward better decision making. Somewhere in that process, we discovered a Taekwondo center not far from our house. The center was geared toward young people (ages 5-15) and seemed to emphasize character skills like respect and discipline. Bingo! We enrolled him immediately. It was an awesome experience and truly connected me with what is important in sports. Yes, they taught physical skills, but the physical element was secondary.

The focus was on building high-character individuals. We never thought about Will becoming a Taekwondo master—it wasn't about that. It was about respect and discipline.

All of the concepts discussed in this book can and should be used with the seven- to nine-year age group. It is not too early for athletes to learn about a growth mindset, self-determination, focusing on controllables, and the importance of building character skills.

The emphasis for this group should definitely be on having a great experience. Any conversations with athletes at this age should lead with, "Are you having fun?" If they are enjoying themselves, they will want to go to practice every day. If they are enjoying themselves, they will want to celebrate with their teammates. If they are enjoying themselves, they will want to work a little harder to improve.

If they are not enjoying themselves, you should dig a little deeper. Are they focusing on controllables? Having fun? Bringing great energy? Being a great teammate? Most often, if they are not having fun, they are simply focused on the wrong things—generally things outside of their control. They may be focused on how many points they're scoring, how many hits they're getting, how they compare to their peers, etc. Even at this age, athletes may focus too much on outcomes. Our society begins to guide young people toward outcomes at a very early age. Grades are an outcome. Points scored are an outcome. We often reward and highlight outcomes, while forgoing chances to reward and highlight effort. Focus your young athlete's attention on effort and all the other controllables. If they have a really good game, tell them that the practice efforts they have been putting in are admirable. If they have a tough game, focus their attention on what they did great within the game and ask them to journal what they want to work on.

Following a game, be sure you close the book on the game as soon as possible. The last thing we want is for our young athlete to be consumed by his or her performance. We do not want our athlete's self-worth to be tied to their sport. Yes, it can start this early. The longer our sons or daughters think about the game, and whether it was good or bad, the more they begin to couple their identity to their sport. As mentioned earlier in the book, this can potentially be damaging down the road.

Age 10-12

I vividly remember a conversation we had with Drew's middle school counselor. This was a planning meeting for Drew's next three years of middle school. Among other questions, the counselor asked Drew what he wanted to be when he grew up. Drew said he wanted to be a professional baseball player. The counselor smirked a little and asked him to pick something more realistic. It took all the mental skills in my toolbox to remain calm. Why would this guy crap on my son's goal? There are professional baseball players, right? It's not impossible, right? After some deep breaths, and a little time to reflect, I came to some conclusions. I assumed that the counselor tied the practicality of Drew becoming a pro baseball player to his lack of work ethic in the classroom. Little did this guy know that Drew would now lean into goal setting, hard work, perseverance, respect, teamwork, and confidence. Becoming a professional athlete takes time, effort, and relentless development as a player and as a person. If Drew wanted to be a professional player, he would learn about all these things.

This is generally the age where thoughts and feelings about what others think of them start to impact young people. These thoughts and feelings can lead to higher levels of anxiety, and can in turn reduce the athletes' joy for the game. Since enjoyment is key (this holds true at any age), we must ensure that our young athletes are not overly concerned with what others are thinking about them. To do this, we once again focus on controllables.

If your young athlete is bringing great energy, being a good teammate, and working hard at practice, that is all anyone can ask of them. We must constantly affirm this with our athletes.

If they are struggling, discuss with them what they are feeling. Do the perceived expectations of others cause them stress and anxiety? If so, reaffirm the controllables. Ask them what they have control over that can guide them toward being the best they can be. Make sure they know that you love them no matter what happens in sports, and that their performance does not, and will never, define who they are as a person. Be sure your son or daughter is staying focused on the character skills they would like to develop. Go through these skills and ask your athlete if they believe that the development of these skills will make them the best player and person they can be.

Many athletes at this age also begin to develop a fear of failure. This fear is developed from the desire to impress others. If they make a mistake, they don't look good. This can contribute to a fixed mindset. They won't try something that might challenge them for fear of messing up and how they would be perceived if they do mess up. We must let our sons and daughters know that mistakes and failures are a huge part of their development. Mistakes and failures can teach us. They teach us what we need to work on. They are not an end point; only a beginning. Many, many young people these days are tormented by the fear of failure. Society teaches them that failure is bad, and that success should come easy. We know this is hogwash. If your son or daughter has some fear-based feelings, focus them on controllables and character skills. The art of focusing on these things is not only great for their development; it can also allow them to feel successful by making them conscious of the progress they are making in these skills.

Age 13-16

When I coached thirteen- through sixteen-year-olds, my biggest focus was teaching them how to play in the present moment: no thoughts about the past, the future, or what their peers were thinking of them. To do this, I had them focus on the controllables and a "we" over "me" attitude.

If it is about us, then what I did in my last at-bat doesn't matter. Only this at-bat matters, *for the team*. If it is all about us, I need to recover from that mistake, and move on, *for the team*. If it is about us, I will do my best to help the team in any way I can. This means it's not just about scoring points. It's about my attitude and energy. We are all equal. We all play a role in our team's successes and failures. When young people feel like they are on an island, pressure and fear can consume them. When they feel like they are part of something bigger, pressure and fear lessen. I always did my best to move guys around in the line-up, move them to different positions in the field, and give them a chance to pitch if they wanted. I wanted each guy to feel that he was an important part of the team.

We also journaled before and after every practice and every game. What did we write down? The things that we could control. We did not control our last at-bat—it's over. We did not control the outcome of this at-bat—only our best effort. We did not control what our peers thought of us—only how we treated them. We controlled our effort, our preparation, our thoughts, and our response to adversity.

I remember the 13AAA state tournament, our last tournament of the season. We were down by two runs in the championship game. We were the home team in the bottom of the seventh (the last) inning. It was our last chance to win the game, with two outs, bases loaded. The last hitter in our line-up was up to bat. The last hitter is generally considered the worst hitter. However, our last hitter had batted all throughout the order all season. Sometimes first, sometimes third, sometimes sixth, and sometimes last. He didn't consider himself any better, or any worse, than any other player on the team. He was just one of the guys. He also journaled, as we all did, before every game. I'm not sure what he wrote in his journal prior to this game, but I'm betting it had something to do with things he could control. He smashed a double that scored three runs, and we walked away champions of the tournament. Do I think he stepped to the plate with a present-minded focus because he was a part of something bigger than himself and was focused on controllables? Yes I do! Did that guarantee him a hit in that situation? Absolutely not...but I sure do think it helped.

Many athletes (and non-athletes) in this age range base their self-worth on how they believe others perceive them. They become concerned about how they have looked in the past and how they will look in the future. These thoughts create stress and anxiety. One common but unfortunate coping mechanism to reduce this stress is avoidance of challenging things (during which they may make mistakes, or even fail). They come to believe that the easiest way to maintain their self-worth (continue to look good) is to avoid challenges. Sadly, by avoiding challenges, they miss great opportunities to learn and grow.

In order to combat the stress created by the desire to look good, we must help guide our sons and daughters toward a growth mindset. We must help them to focus on controllables and we must highlight character development.

This age group can become very thoughtful and insightful in their journaling. They are beginning to become more insightful about their emotions and how their emotions can affect their desired outcomes. Be sure your sons and daughters are writing down how they are feeling during their practices and games. These feelings can create insights into solutions that can guide them toward improvements in performance.

Here is an example:

Following his game, John writes down that he felt stressed and anxious while at the free throw line. You discuss with John why he felt stressed. John says he was stressed because he really wanted to make the two free throws. This reply from John is totally understandable. You then ask John if he is one hundred percent in control of making his free throws. He says yes; he thinks he is in control. You then ask him if Steph Curry makes all of his free throws. "Well, no, he does not." "Well, John, if Steph Curry doesn't make all his free throws, why should you?" Young athletes often think they are in control of their outcomes. They should make every shot, get a hit every time, etc. They want to be in control, but they are not. So we have to take a step back with John. Focus him on what he does control in his free throws: a deep breath, 3 dribbles, and his final thought.

Let me stress here that we can't simply wish away stressful thoughts. In fact, research shows that trying to think about getting rid of negative thoughts only strengthens those thoughts. We must therefore create new thoughts. Thoughts that displace the negative. This of course is way easier said than done, but with patience, and more practice, it can be done.

A young athlete learning to understand what he or she can and cannot control is a huge step, and is sometimes enough to reduce stress and anxiety. As parents, we can also be more mindful about what they do and don't control. We often get upset when our sons or daughters don't perform well, but we should be focusing on their controllables and their character development. Were they a good teammate? Did they have good energy? Did they respond well to adversity? These should be the areas of focus for us as parents.

Another stressor that develops in athletes around this age is personal expectations. They expect certain outcomes. They undoubtedly have had some success, and they begin to believe they should have that success on a regular basis. These personal expectations should be met with goal setting, the "why," and the "how" for achieving their goals. It's great if they begin to set higher standards for their outcomes, but if they focus solely on the outcomes, they will begin to ride a roller coaster of emotions (as great outcomes inevitably come and go), and in turn their overall experience will suffer.

As parents, we must be sure our sons and daughters are focused on the right things. The "why" and the "how" are the right things.

Age 17+

Around this age, many athletes begin to think about "what's next." They are beginning to consider where their sport might take them, or how they might feel if they aren't playing anymore. Pressure due to personal expectations and the perceived expectations of others are likely still in play. On top of those concerns, we can now add anxious thoughts about the future.

Reducing the "what's next" pressure is no different than tackling other sorts of pressure. Focus on character development and controllables. Athletes should journal when they are feeling overwhelmed with pressure. In what situations do they feel increased pressure? Acknowledging these situations can give them a heads-up to when they may feel this pressure. That heads-up can lead them toward ways to combat the pressure. "When I feel stressed prior to a game, I will journal my controllables, take two deep breaths, and focus on my pre-game routine."

Another problem that arises within this age group is the thought that they should no longer feel stress or anxiety. They think that if they show any signs of stress, they will appear weak. As parents, we must be aware of this. We must have good conversations with our sons and daughters about how they are feeling. We must move past the "How did your day go?" conversations and really work to find out how they are doing. Ask them more specific questions. "How is math class going?" "How are you getting along with your teammates?" "What are your goals for the season?" We need to dig a little deeper. Stress and anxiety levels have never been higher in teenagers than they are today. We must help our sons and daughters navigate their emotions.

CHAPTER 9

DEALING WITH PRESSURE

"Through breathing and positive self-talk, I have found a version of myself where I am the strongest and most confident."

— Courtney Hennen,
Prior Lake H.S., Softball

There are several sources of pressure. In this chapter, we will look at where pressure comes from and discover tools for dealing with pressure.

Let me say first that pressure is a perception, and it is important to recognize that the athlete's perception of pressure is what matters. Some athletes will perceive zero pressure when they are at bat with the bases loaded, while others will perceive tons of pressure. I think it is important to note this for a couple of reasons:

1. In the past, I have told athletes that there is no need to feel pressure in this situation or that situation. I have told them it is no big deal (when the bases are loaded with two outs in the last inning). I have told them to relax and do

their best. It's a good thought, but it doesn't help. They are feeling the pressure. They are perceiving this to be a critical situation. Now they feel even worse because I am telling them they shouldn't be feeling nervous, but they are! They start wondering if something is wrong with them. "Dang, I'm nervous, but the coach says I shouldn't be nervous. What's wrong with me?" I don't take this approach anymore. If they are feeling pressure, we must give them techniques to deal with the pressure, rather than telling them to ignore it.

2. Athletes need to know that they can learn to control their response to pressure. If they perceive pressure as something outside of their control, they will certainly succumb to it. If they know they can control their response to pressure, they feel in control when pressure heightens.

Where Does Pressure Come From?
Internal Expectations

These are expectations created from within. "I expect to score 20 points." "I expect to get 3 hits." "I expect to be one of the best players on the team."

Most young athletes that are passionate about their sport have high internal expectations. This is totally normal and can even be useful at times. If they are passionate about their sport, they will be driven to succeed. They will have goals and expect to reach those goals. They will work hard to reach their goals. Again, this can be a good thing, but there is definitely a downside to certain types of internal expectations.

By this point in the book, you can undoubtedly see the downside of internal expectations based on outcome goals. Because outcome goals are generally based on factors outside of our control, there is no guarantee of success. The athlete ends up riding a roller coaster of emotions. They feel great when they reach their desired outcome; they feel disappointed when they don't. This roller coaster can lead to persistent negative thoughts, which can decrease their love for their sport.

Another problem that can potentially arise with outcome-based expectations is a lack of a sense of accomplishment even when goals are reached. They expect to score twenty points, so it doesn't feel rewarding when they do. We want them to feel pleasure in their success and not be constantly chasing the result. Often this type of chase can also lead to a decrease in development. If they are only focused on the outcome, they can lose opportunities for character growth. Character is built through focused character development. When there is a constant chase for results, character development can get left behind. So many lessons can be learned when a young person is engaged in pursuing their process goals. A chase for outcomes robs them of their process.

External Expectations

Perceived pressure from teammates, coaches, and parents can overwhelm a young athlete. Similar to internal expectations, these perceived pressures are generally outcome-based, and therefore outside of the athlete's control. "My teammates expect me to score twenty points." "My coach expects me to lead the team in hits." "My dad expects me to throw three touchdowns and lead our team to victory."

Again, these and similar expectations are outcome-based, and outside of the athlete's control. To reiterate, if an athlete does not feel in control of what they are trying to accomplish, they will feel stress, anxiety, and pressure.

We must refrain from adding pressure to our athlete's already full plate. We must discuss controllables. We must allow room for mistakes and help them work through ways to recover and move on from mistakes. Following games, we must focus on controllables. Energy, effort, physical skills they can control, and so on.

Past Experiences

"I struck out my last at-bat." "I missed my last shot." "I don't want to fail again." "I haven't gotten a hit in two games."

Negative thoughts from the past can plant seeds of doubt and negativity. The brain can only process one thought at a time. If that thought is guided by past negative experiences, it becomes impossible to focus on what is important right now. If an athlete is still reeling from his last at-bat, thinking about how poorly it went, he will struggle mightily to find confidence for this at-bat.

An athlete must have the ability to be in the present moment. After all, this pitch, this shot, this pass, is really all that matters. The skill of being in the present moment is undoubtedly one of the most important, if not the most important, mental skill.

Before diving into techniques to be in the present moment, let's first look at one other source of pressure.

Thoughts About the Future

"I hope I get a hit here." "I hope I make this shot." "I hope I don't fail here." The problem here is that all these thoughts about the future are outcome-based and uncontrollable. Uncontrollable equals added pressure. If the thoughts about the future were, "I will give full energy to this play," "I will take my best swings this at-bat," and, "I will play intense defense this time down the floor," perceptions surrounding failure would disappear.

Athletes must learn that they do not have control of many of the outcomes they hope for. Yes, they can do A, B, and C to give them the best chance of getting a hit, but they don't control whether or not they get a hit.

Techniques For Dealing with Pressure

The following are skills that any athlete can use to deal with perceived pressure. Note that certain athletes prefer certain skills over others. Go through each of these skills with your son or daughter. Ask them which skills they think they might find useful. Then let them have at it.

These skills must be practiced! Mental skills are just like physical skills. In order for them to show up in a game, they must be practiced. Yelling, "Slow down and take a deep breath!" is meaningless to an athlete that has no idea what a calming breath feels like.

Routines

My son Will's first two games at Arizona State University did not go the way he had envisioned. In the first game, batting clean-up, he went 0-4 with 2 strikeouts. In the second game, he was dropped in the batting order to sixth. He went 0-2 with 2 strikeouts. Needless to say, he was a bit frustrated. Then came the third game. He went 3-5, with 2 HR's (one of which was a grand slam), 1 2B, and 6 RBI. Following the game, a reporter asked him if he had made any adjustments. Will said that in the first two games he had felt pretty anxious and was not able to be in the present moment. He discussed how he was able to be present in his routines for the last game. He said that prior to the game he listened to the music on the stadium loudspeakers and enjoyed being with his teammates. He said that during the game, when he was on-deck, he was where his feet were (a term for being in the present moment), focusing his gaze and intentions on the pitcher.

Using routines can be one of the most straightforward techniques for dealing with pressure. Most athletes already have routines, so directing their minds toward a sharpened focus on their routines can be easier than some of the other techniques.

The first step in this process is to ask them to be mindful of their routines. Athletes have routines for everything. They have pre-game routines and they have in-game routines. Routines are simply things athletes do over and over again. An example of a pre-game routine would be a warm-up. Generally, athletes go through the same, or close to the same, warm-up routine before each game. An example of an in-game routine varies from sport to sport. In baseball, an example of an in-game routine would be a batter's box routine, such as taking a deep breath, digging the back foot into the dirt, and thinking positive thoughts. In basketball, it would be a free throw line routine, such as taking a deep breath, bouncing the ball twice, and thinking positive thoughts. The key to making these routines tools for reducing stress is getting the athlete fully engaged in their routine. If they are fully engaged in their routine and completely mindful of what they are doing, their thoughts cannot be on things that create anxiety.

To be totally present in their routines, they should be aware of their senses. What do they see? What do they hear? What do they smell? What are they touching? See, hear, smell, touch. This may seem like a lot to consider, but as I said earlier, they are already doing routines—we just want them to be mindful of what they are doing. Each athlete may choose to call on different senses as part of their routines. For Will, he engaged his hearing (listening to the music), and his sight and hearing (having fun with teammates), prior to the game. During the game, when he was on deck, he engaged his sight once again as he focused on the pitcher.

Ask your athlete to be aware of what they are seeing, hearing, smelling, and/or touching during their routines. As they work through this, they should write in their journal what senses are engaged during their routines. "During pre-game, when I'm warming up, I like to smell the grass, listen to my teammates, and feel the ground under my feet." "During the game, when I'm in the batter's box, I like to feel the grip of my bat and look over the entire field." Once they are aware of which senses they engage in, they should be aware of those senses each and every time they go through their routines. If they are engaging in these senses, their thoughts cannot be engaged elsewhere.

There are two components an athlete can add to sharpen their focus even further when they are using routines to reduce stress. The first is an awareness of their energy levels, and the second is an awareness of their thoughts.

When considering energy, the focus needs to be on having an awareness of an energy level that makes them feel most ready to compete. One question needs to be answered by the athlete: "What is your optimal energy level for competition?" To do this, I'll recommend to athletes to use a scale from one to ten, where one is sleeping and ten is totally hyped. Where do they want to be on this scale when they are competing? This varies from one athlete to another (personal preference). Some baseball players like to be super hyped; maybe they want to be at a nine or ten on the scale. Others like to be more calm; maybe they want to be at a five or six. Athletes in different sports can have different levels (a football player would generally be higher on the scale, while a golfer would be lower). When your son or daughter decides what level of energy is best for them, they should write that level in their journal. It is great for them to have this in their journal so they can revisit it prior to competition.

Once the athlete knows where they want to be on the one to ten scale, they must then be able to recognize when they are not at that level. When they can manage these first two steps, they can make adjustments to get themselves to the level they desire.

A great way to work through the entire process of recognizing where their energy levels are, and then making adjustments accordingly, is using a technique called "body scanning." A body scan is simply taking a minute to check in with the body. Where is my energy level at this very moment? When the athlete is going through their pre-game routine, they stop for a minute, do a body scan, and ask themselves where their energy level is. If their energy is low, they work to bring it up. To do this, they can ramp up the physical part of their pre-game routine, use self-talk to raise their energy ("I gotta crank it up!"), or they can use a breathing technique described in the upcoming "breathing" section titled "breathing for energy." If energy levels are too high when they do a body scan, they can slow the pace of their pre-game routine, use self-talk to lower energy levels ("I need to slow things down a bit"), or they can use a breathing technique described in the upcoming "breathing" section titled "breathing for calm."

For in-game routines, the athlete should go through the same process they used with their pre-game routines. In game, they should find times when they commonly need to check in on their energy levels (do a body scan). Baseball and softball batters might do a body scan when they are on deck or in the hole. Baseball and softball pitchers might do a body scan right before they get on the mound to start an inning. Basketball players might do a body scan when they're at the free throw line.

The second piece to consider when using routines to deal with anxiety is the mental piece. The mental piece is just a slight addition to everything described above. The first step in the mental piece is the athlete becoming aware of what thoughts are useful to them. What thoughts do they want filling their minds when they take the field, court, etc.? To become more mindful of these thoughts, the athlete should write in their journal the thoughts they want to carry with them into competition. They may write things like "fun," "excited," "relaxed," etc. Once they know what thoughts are useful to them, they can recognize when they are not having those thoughts. Now when they do their body scan during their routines, they simply check in on their thoughts. If they are having positive thoughts, great—carry on. If they are having negative thoughts, they should stop and use the 3 R's (outlined on page 36), reframing (outlined on page 85), self-talk (outlined on page 86), or useful thinking (outlined on page 88) to get them back on track.

Now let's pull this all together. The athlete knows the energy level at which they want to compete. They know the thoughts they want to carry into competition. As they go through their routines, they do a body scan to check in on their energy and thoughts. If both are good, they proceed to compete. If one or the other or both are off, they make the necessary adjustments before continuing to compete.

That's a lot to take in. But using routines to help reduce pressure is really just about the athlete being aware of their surroundings, their energy, and their thoughts. Self-awareness is a great thing!

Breathing

When an athlete is focused completely on their breath, they are in the present moment. The ability to be in the present moment brings focus to the task at hand with no distractions. This calms the mind. There are no worries about the past, the future, the scoreboard, or anyone's expectations. Breathing focuses and calms the mind. Breathing can also calm the body. When an athlete has anxiety, the result is generally tension in the body. Proper breathing can help relieve this physical tension, which is why breathing can calm both the mind and the body.

There are many, many breathing techniques. I recommend finding simple techniques that can be used in many situations and are easily accessed by the athlete. You and your son or daughter can easily do a Google search of breathing techniques to find one they like and will use. I generally recommend two types of breathing. The first is for calm (if the athlete is nervous or anxious), and the second is for energy (if the athlete is tired or lethargic).

Breathing For Calm

The key to breathing for calm is smooth and controlled breathing. The 4-7-8 technique is considered one of the best. 4-second inhale through the nose, 7-second hold, and 8-second exhale through the mouth. The breath should go into the belly and out from the belly.

Breathing for Energy

The key to breathing for energy is a forceful exhale. A simple technique that I teach is a slow 3-second inhale (through the nose), a 1-second hold, and a forceful exhale (through the mouth with pursed lips), followed immediately by a second forceful exhale.

In baseball, between pitches, a batter does not have enough time to take 20 seconds to breathe. In instances like this, the athlete should find a breathing pattern that works best for them. Maybe it's 2-2-2, or something similar. Again, for calming breaths, the key is to be smooth and controlled with the inhale and exhale, and for energy, the key is to have a smooth inhale and a forceful exhale.

A secondary benefit of focused breathing, as well as any of these techniques for being present, is the benefit of taking focus away from negative thoughts. If the athlete is focused on breathing, what else can they be thinking about? Nothing.

Breathing is a skill that must be practiced. I have heard coaches and parents yell to an athlete "Breathe!" Unless the athlete has practiced breathing, and feels a sense of calm from breathing, just yelling "breathe" does little to no good.

Laughter

Yes, laughter. Many athletes look for fun and laughter when they are feeling pressure. Laughing allows the athlete to be in the present moment. They're enjoying teammates, coaches, and playing the game. Laughter has the benefit of making perceived pressures feel less intense. Shoot, if I can laugh about it, how much pressure can there be? Athletes should find outlets for laughter before, during, and after games.

Music

Music can serve to reduce perceived pressure prior to games, during games (depending on the sport), and after games. For many young athletes, their music is a way to escape the pressures of the game.

Meditation

Meditation can seem scary and awkward for many athletes, but it can be simple and straightforward. For me, mediation is simply the art of clearing the mind. We want to eliminate distractions and bring ourselves into the present moment so we can then move forward. When I go through mediations with my athletes, I simply remind them, "We're doing this to clear the mind." Saying this seems to give them the freedom to relax and take on the process. I generally use three types of mediation with my clients. The first is a calming meditation (used if nerves or excitement levels are too high). The second is used to increase levels of energy (if an athlete is feeling tired or lethargic). The third is active mediation (if an athlete needs or wants to be moving during mediation). As with breathing, you can simply Google search "mediation" and find many, many different forms. The key is to find something that works for your son or daughter.

In the following meditation examples, I am using what is called "unguided meditation." "Guided" meditation is a meditation that is led by someone, while "unguided" is self-led. I have chosen to use unguided so your athlete can have access to mediation at any time and won't need someone to take them through the meditation practice.

Meditation for calm (takes about 5 minutes). The athlete should find a place where they can sit or lie comfortably. The mediation begins with breathing. Your son or daughter needs to take one or two minutes to focus on and connect with their breathing. They should breathe at their own pace. Next, they can start at the bottom of their body, relaxing each muscle group as they work their way up the body. Relax the feet. Relax the calves. Relax the quads. Relax the hamstrings. Relax the glutes. Relax the abs. Relax the low back. Relax the chest. Relax the upper back. Relax the shoulders. Relax the upper arm. Relax the forearms. Relax the hands. Relax the neck. Relax the face. Relax the top of their head. Let their body sink into the floor. If at any point their mind wanders from the relaxing of their muscles, they should simply recognize the wandering thoughts and pull themselves back to the relaxation of their muscles. When they have reached the top of their head, they should stay in this state for a minute or so. Once they are ready, they should reconnect with their breathing and slowly bring themselves back to an externally-aware state.

Meditation for energy (takes about 5 minutes). The athlete should find a place where they can sit or lie comfortably. They should take one or two minutes to focus on and connect with their breathing. They should breathe at their own pace. Once they feel comfortable with their breath, similar to calming meditation, they should begin to work up their body. This time though, they should think about their breath reaching each muscle and supplying that muscle with energy. First the feet—filling the feet with oxygen and energy. Then the calves. The quads. The hamstrings. The glutes. The low back. The abs. As they go, they are filling each muscle with oxygen and energy. The chest. The upper back. The shoulders. The upper arms. The forearms. The hands. The neck. The face. The top of the head. Now they can feel oxygen and energy flow throughout the body. They should stay in this state for one or two minutes. After one or two minutes, they should reconnect with their smooth, energy-filled breath, and when they are ready, they can bring themselves back to an externally-aware state.

Active Meditation. There are situations when finding space to be still and quiet can be hard for an athlete (during practice, pre-game, or game). There are also athletes that prefer the flow of movement during meditation. Active mediation can fill the needs of both of these groups.

Active meditation is the art of being present in whatever they are doing. If they are stretching, they should be deliberate about focusing on each stretch. If they are doing layups, they should be deliberate about focusing on each layup.

Like meditation for calm and meditation for energy, active meditation starts with the breath. The athlete should center their thoughts on their breathing. If the athlete is trying to bring a sense of calm, they should use a slow inhale and a slow exhale. If the athlete is trying to create energy, they should use a slow inhale and a forceful exhale (see calming and energy breathing above). The athlete can take a few seconds to lock in on their breathing between reps if they are doing an activity that allows it (e.g. playing catch), or they can connect with their breath while doing the activity (e.g. during an active warm up). Once the athlete has connected with their breath, they should begin to hone in on their senses. First, they can connect with the muscles throughout their body (feeling them relax if they are feeling anxious, or feeling them fill with energy if they are feeling lethargic). What are their feet doing? What are their lower legs doing? What are their upper legs doing? What are their abdominal muscles and lower back doing? What is their upper back doing? What are their arms doing? Next, they can connect with their smell. What are they smelling? Then they can connect with their hearing. What are they hearing? Next, they can connect with their touch. What are they touching? Lastly, they can connect with their sight. What are they seeing? The athlete then takes one final deep breath, and they have completed their active meditation.

I know this can sound like a lot, but with practice, it only needs to take a few minutes. Here is an example of what it might look like: John is playing catch prior to a game and is feeling anxious (he needs to feel a sense of calm). Between reps of catch, he connects with his breath. He slowly inhales and slowly exhales. He then works his way up his body, feeling a sense of relaxation in each muscle group. John then takes a minute to connect with his smell, taking a few good inhales. He then connects with his hearing, listening closely to the sounds around him. John then connects with his touch. He feels the glove in his hands, and the baseball as he is about to throw it. Lastly, John connects with his sight. He sees his catch partner, his teammates, the grass, the outfield fence, etc. John takes one final deep and calming breath, and he has completed his active meditation.

Journaling

When an athlete writes down their controllable goals for a practice or a game, the physical and mental and character goals they are working on, they are bringing themselves into the present. They are identifying what is important to them right now. Where should they direct their attention? What do they control? No distractions.

Focal Point

When an athlete focuses their eyes and thoughts on a fixed point, putting their total attention on that fixed point, they can be thinking of nothing else, so they are then in the present. Different athletes use a variety of things as their focal points, and they use them in different ways and at different times in the game.

Some players like to use a focal point during their pre-game. They may look at the scoreboard, check out all the details of the board, or see the lights, the words, etc. Doing this in their pre-game can bring a sense of calm.

Some players like to have a focal point as part of their in-game routines. Many batters will stare at some lettering on their bat between pitches, focusing their eyes and their thoughts only on those words. Doing this can bring a sense of calm between each pitch.

Grounding

Grounding is simply feeling your feet on the ground. Many athletes feel present simply by "grounding," or pushing their feet into the ground, floor, field, ice, etc. In baseball, batters do this all the time when they "dig" into the batter's box. Even though they might not know it, they are often "grounding" themselves into the at-bat. They are getting themselves into the present moment, where only this pitch matters. Basketball players might do it at the free throw line. Golfers might do it as they get into their stance.

Recognizing the Need to Be Present

This is the hardest piece of the presence puzzle. Most athletes don't recognize when they are not present until it is too late. Things speed up on them. They become overly excited, anxious, etc. For untrained athletes, the mind can spiral out of control before they ever know what happened. You've seen it. Things seem fine, then one bad thing happens and the athlete immediately goes to a bad place. The tricky part is that our emotional brain usually "drives the bus." Our emotional brain becomes immediately alerted when something negative happens, and it wants to respond right away. Yes, the same thing happens to us adults. Think of the last time something bad happened to you. Did you immediately respond poorly? Did you immediately choose a good and helpful response? Generally, our immediate response is driven by emotions and is a poor response. However, if we understand this, and if we allow ourselves a few seconds to get control of our emotions, we can then choose a good response. This is no different for athletes. An umpire makes a bad call. The athlete's immediate emotional response will probably not be good. However, if the athlete takes a second, steps out of the box, and collects his or her thoughts, they can then choose a good response. The good response comes from the rational mind. But again, the emotional mind is the first thing we access—the rational mind needs a little time to respond.

A huge part of an athlete's recognition that they might be unable to stay present is the ability to know when negative or unhelpful thoughts are likely to occur. This is planning ahead. Journaling is a great tool for this. If, after a game, the athlete writes down the situation when negative thoughts crept in, they can then plan for a better response if it happens again. Consider the example of the bad umpire call. When a tough call went against Johnny, he reacted poorly. He hung his head and got really upset. Johnny couldn't stop thinking about the bad call and that at-bat, and for the rest of the game, he didn't play very well. Following the game, Johnny wrote down what happened. He also wrote down that the next time he gets a bad call, he will react differently. He will step out of the batter's box, take a deep calming breath, ground himself back in the box, and take his best swing.

Reframing

Reframing is taking a thought or perception about something and reframing it to look at it in a different light. We all know people who are very positive. We also know people who are very negative. The positive person can look at a certain situation and see the upside. The negative person can look at the same situation and see the downside. Why is that? Yes, there are often past experiences that lead to the decision to be positive or negative, but do these past experiences necessarily dictate what will happen this time around? No, they do not. The ability to reframe is incredibly powerful. I'll often use the phrase, "Is this an obstacle or an opportunity?" We can help our young athletes to see the opportunities in front of them, even when things seem hard...especially when things seem hard.

An example of reframing is changing perceptions on stress. The body's responses to "stress" and "excitement" are very similar: increased heart rate, tense muscles, and chest breathing. I will often ask young athletes whether they are stressed, nervous, or maybe just excited. We tend to believe that our thoughts control our bodies, but often our actions (bodies) can control our thoughts. Let me explain. A young athlete's heart rate increases and their breathing gets faster. They then immediately relate this body arousal to stress or nervousness. But is their body's arousal necessarily due to stress? No, it is not. Maybe they are appropriately excited—excited for what is about to happen. Once an athlete understands this, they can reframe their thoughts. "I am excited to play today!" Thinking they are excited rather than nervous can change everything for them. "Stressed" or "nervous" have negative connotations; "excited" does not.

Self-Talk

Self-talk can be very powerful. We spend all day talking to ourselves. The question is, what are we saying? Studies have shown that about 80% of our self-talk is negative. Wait, what?! Yes, 80% negative. Imagine the changes we could make in our lives if we could flip this to 80% positive!

Awareness is the key. How do I generally speak to myself? In what specific situations do I tend to negatively speak to myself? Answers to these two questions can bring about self-awareness.

Most people have a general way in which they speak to themselves. Check in with your son or daughter. Ask them how they speak to themselves. Ask them to be aware of, and journal, negative things they say to themselves. Awareness of how they speak to themselves is step one. Ask them how negative self-talk benefits them. There are very few, if any, good answers to this question.

There are also specific situations where we may be more likely to engage in negative self-talk. It could be around specific people, or when we're faced with a challenge. Ask your son or daughter to be aware of these situations and to write about them in their journal.

Journaling when they engage in negative self-talk helps bring awareness to it. It also helps them to plan for situations where they may find themselves in a negative place. If they are able to have a plan going into those situations, it will be easier for them to navigate through the situations.

The second step is replacing the negative self-talk with positive or useful (discussed in the next section) self-talk. Instead of "I can't do this," it might be "I can't do this yet." Instead of "I suck," it might be "I'm not good at this yet." The word "yet" can be very powerful. It gives us a chance to succeed, if we put in the work. Talk with your son or daughter about adding the word "yet" to their vocabulary!

I can think of many situations in sports where negative self-talk is likely to occur. Prior to games (when athletes are unsure of how they will do), after making a mistake, when the team is struggling, in the on-deck circle (nervous about getting a hit), and many, many more. Again, your son or daughter should recognize situations that may lead them into negative self-talk, and have a plan to attack them with positive, or useful, self-talk.

I don't recommend fake positive self-talk, or self-talk that focuses the athlete on things outside of their control. Fake positive self-talk would be telling themselves things they do not really believe. For example, saying something like, "I'm going to score 40 points tonight," when they truly know they will not. Keep it real. The brain knows when we are telling it lies. If the brain knows we're lying, it won't give us the full effort we're asking for. Self-talk that focuses on something outside of the athlete's control might be, "I'm going to get a hit here." In this instance, what happens if they don't get a hit? Now they don't believe that positive person in their head. Better self-talk in this instance would be, "I'm going to take my best swings in this at-bat."

You can learn a lot about your son's or daughter's self-talk when they are verbalizing their thoughts. Pay attention to what they say about themselves out loud. It is very likely that if they are negative toward themselves out loud, they are also negative within. If you hear your son or daughter verbalizing negativity, call their attention to it. Again, awareness is key.

Useful Thinking

When I first started working with young athletes, I would try to get them to switch from a negative mindset to a positive one. Maybe an athlete had just struck out with the bases loaded and I'd say, "Keep your head up; stay positive." For many athletes, this never worked. And in retrospect, why would it? Striking out sucks! Now, I instead discuss useful thinking.

Useful thinking is not positive or negative. It is a way of thinking with a present moment focus. Useful thinking recognizes that something good, or bad, just happened, but what is important either way is that we next move on to the best step forward. An example: Billy just struck out. Billy can take a few seconds to be upset. He then shifts his thoughts to what he needs to do to move forward. "I need to get on the fence and cheer on my teammates." Or, "I will have great energy when I take the field." These thoughts don't need to be positive, but they do need to be productive. Negative thinking is not productive. Useful thinking says it's okay to be upset, and now let's move forward.

CHAPTER 10

TROPHIES FOR EVERYONE!

"It's easy to get lost in the world of instant gratification, but that's never the reason you play or compete."

— Brett Bateman,
Chicago Cubs Minor League Baseball

Several years ago, the number of participants in youth sports began to decline. Part of the problem was thought to be a lack of competence that many young athletes were feeling (I'm not good enough). Handing out trophies to only the top teams or top athletes made some of the other athletes feel insignificant. If they weren't good enough, why should they participate? The solution often implemented was to offer "participation" trophies to any and all competitors. Now, everyone will feel good!

There are a few problems with the reward-for-participation model. The first problem is that an athlete who knows they will receive a reward, no matter what, has no incentive to put in any effort. Why should they work hard if they'll get a trophy either way? Within this system, we are teaching young people that effort does not matter. Sadly, I think this has created a widely-held misconception among today's youth. Many of them have been led to believe they are owed something with no regard to their effort or performance.

The flip side of the athlete that decides it's not necessary to make the effort is the athlete that does work hard. In the reward-for-participation model, what is their reward? They see athletes who just show up get a trophy. How is that fair? Now they can become frustrated, and may even decide to cut corners in their own work. "I'm a hard worker, but only the outcome matters (the trophy), so I won't kill myself." This athlete is then moving toward a fixed mindset: it's not the effort that matters; it's the outcome.

Another problem with the reward-for-participation model is a physiological factor. When we feel a sense of accomplishment, our brains release a chemical called dopamine. Dopamine is like an addictive drug: the more we feel the pleasure from it, the more we crave it. A dopamine release can certainly be a good thing. It can intensify our craving to reach a goal. When we reach a goal, and dopamine is released, we feel amazing. The downside of the reward-for-participation system is that the dopamine will only be released when we get the reward. The reward is the only goal, so dopamine will only be released when we get a trophy. In contrast, if we are truly engaged in the process, if we are engaged in the steps to move our needle toward our goals, we will get dopamine releases along the way. We will accomplish small goals along the way, getting a release of dopamine each time we navigate an obstacle. This is the model we want young people to engage in. I take a step forward, dopamine is released, and I feel great. I overcome adversity, dopamine is released, and I feel great. We are engaged in the present moment, not focused solely on a reward that will come in the future.

Both of my sons wrestled. Wrestling is as physically and mentally demanding as any sport. The physicality is no joke. Wrestlers work their tails off: running, push-ups, sit-ups, and one-on-one battles every practice. As difficult as the physical component is, the mental component is even more challenging. When they lose, there is only one person accountable. They can either quit or get better. And there is only one way to get better: put in the work. So many great lessons!

At youth levels in wrestling, every participant gets an award. In wrestling, I thought this was fair. Maybe there were some kids out there that didn't work hard, but I didn't see them. If you can make it through the grueling practices, you deserve an award. There were almost always tiered podiums that the kids would stand on after receiving their awards (mostly set up so the parents could take pictures). The top finisher would stand on the highest tier, and they knew they were the champion. At first, my kids felt good winning any award at a tournament. Whether they won first, second, or third place, it didn't matter. They were proud. However, after a few years, they didn't want the second or third place award. They knew the only way to get that first place award was through hard work.

All of the coaches my kids had for wrestling were former wrestlers. They understood what it took to compete in wrestling. I don't think I ever heard them talk to the kids about winning. They knew that winning was a byproduct of hard work. They knew that the kids were giving their best. For these coaches, the awards didn't matter.

CHAPTER 11

COACHING YOUR SON OR DAUGHTER

"One of the greatest things my dad taught me was to "not believe the hype." What he meant by that was to keep your head down and keep grinding."

— *Brett Bateman,*
Chicago Cubs Minor League Baseball

Coaching my sons has been one of the most challenging and rewarding things I have done in my life. Navigating the two sides of this coin can be both exhausting and exhilarating. I have had many ups and downs in this process. Through my experiences, both good and bad, I have learned many things. I believe the lessons I have learned can help any parent-coach build a strong relationship with their son or daughter.

You are a parent first. Yes, wear your coaching hat when you are a coach. But never forget your number one responsibility: being a parent. There have definitely been times when I have forgotten this. I have slipped into "coaching mode" and have stayed in that mode on the car ride home, during supper, and into the evening. At some point, we must take off the coaching hat. Our sons and daughters do not want to be coached twenty-four hours a day.

They want to be coached during practices and games. They want to do other things when they are off the field. My sons love baseball, but no one wants to do something all of the time. I have learned that stepping away from the game is as important as practice. When we step away, we come back to the game with more passion. At some point, I don't remember exactly when, I decided that when the practices or games ended, the coaching ended. I let my sons know that I was always available, but when the practice or game ended, I was done coaching. Separating these two takes effort, it still does, but there is nothing more valuable as a parent-coach. Communicate this to your son or daughter: When we're on the field, I'm your coach. When we're off the field, I'm your parent.

On the field, your son or daughter should be treated like any of your players. They should all get equal time and equal coaching. This can be hard. I have often wondered whether I am unfairly giving more coaching to my sons, or overcompensating by not giving them as much. I have relied on other coaches to help guide me on this. I simply ask my fellow coaches whether they see me giving equal coaching to all the players, including my sons.

I have also asked other coaches to take the lead in coaching my sons. One year, I made an agreement with a dad with whom I was coaching. He would always speak to my son when I was upset, and I would always speak to his son when he was upset. That was probably the single smartest thing I ever did on the field. To this day, we thank each other almost every time we see each other. We trusted each other to have some hard conversations with our sons. Doing it this way ensured a coach-to-player conversation and never a parent-to-player conversation.

Always focus on controllables. If you can do this, you will have a great relationship. Is this hard? Yes. I have been frustrated when one of my sons goes 0-4. But with patience and practice,

I have grown much better at letting go of the 0-4 games. How have I done this? I have one simple question I ask my sons: "How did you do in the areas you control?" This is what we want to think about. If we can focus on controllable ways to improve, we are teaching them a growth mindset. This keeps them coming back for more. It pushes them to become great teammates and leaders. It teaches them that development comes with time and effort. So, how was their energy? How was their effort? How did they respond to adversity? Were they in control of their emotions? Were they a great teammate? Challenge them in these areas. The more you challenge them in these areas, the more this becomes a way of life, for both you and your child.

Journaling has made the single biggest difference in my relationships with my sons. They write down their controllable goals for the season, why these goals are important, and how they will achieve their goals. They write down the character skills they want to develop, why these skills are important to them, and the daily behaviors they need to take to build these skills. This gives us a definitive focus, each and every day.

Pre-game and pre-practice, they will journal their controllable goals for the day: great energy, great teammates, great approach at the plate, recovering quickly after a mistake, etc. This gives us controllable things to focus on and work toward. It eliminates concerns about things outside of their control—for them, and also for me.

Post-game, they journal the things they did well. "I was a great teammate today. I picked up Johnny after his mistake in the field." "When the umpire made a tough third strike call on me, I released it on my way back to the dugout and supported my teammates immediately." They also journal the things they want to work on. "I struggled with two strikes today. I want to get better at two-strike hitting." "I had a hard time recovering when I got called out on strikes. I need to get better at recovering faster." After they journal, I will simply ask them if there are things they would like to talk about. If they say no, we move on to other things. If they say yes, we'll discuss whatever they want to talk about. Are there times when they do not bring up things that I see? Yes, there are. I have to then ask myself if what I see is really worth talking about right after the game. If it is something they need to work on, why bring it up right after the game? It can wait until the next day, or the next time we go out and practice.

I journal pre-practice, post-practice, pre-game, in-game, and post-game. An obvious reason to do this is to lead by example. If it's important for my sons, it should be important for me.

Journaling pre-practice and pre-game helps me focus on controllables. "Today, no matter what, I will only give positive feedback to my players," "Today I will have great energy throughout the game," etc. I may also journal specific things I need to focus on with my son for that day. "I will be sure to give Will only positive feedback today." "Remind Drew to do a body scan when he's on deck."

During games, to hold myself accountable, I'll often re-visit the controllables I wrote down prior to the game. I'll also write down controllable highlights I'm seeing from the players that I want to mention after the game. Things like high-energy plays, situations where a player overcame adversity, etc. I will also make notes of things I want to work on at upcoming practices. If needed, I'll write down things I want to talk to my son about. These things are always the controllable ones: the controllable things he did well and the controllable things I think he needs to work on.

Post-game and post-practice, I'll reflect on what I did well and what I need to work on. This process has been a game changer for me. Prior to journaling, my emotions often ran high after games, with thoughts swirling in my head about this or that. Journaling after games has given me a chance to slow down. I'll take some time to really reflect on what's important. Was this one game that important? What did we learn from this game? How did I do with the controllables? How did the players do with the controllables?

After the game, if I'm with my son, I'll ask him if he wants to share things he wrote in his journal. If he does, great. If he doesn't, there is a good chance his emotions are high, so we'll do it another time. If he is sharing, I'll ask if I can share my thoughts (that I journaled during the game) with him. Again, if he says okay, great. If he says no, then it's not the right time.

As coaches, we often see many things that the players need to work on. Post-game is not the right time to go through this list. Emotions are high, for us and for the players. I learned this pretty early on, when one of my players actually brought it to my attention: "Coach, you talk too much after the games." I asked my son if he agreed, and he did. I began to simply ask the players after the games if they had anything to share. Sometimes they did, and other times they didn't. The only other things I would mention after games were any positive things I saw. These would always be the controllable things. "Johnny responded great after giving up the double." "Billy was working really hard in pre-game on his opposite field swing." Highlight controllables, and be specific about what you are highlighting. If your players know you are looking for certain things, they will work to achieve those things. If you highlight performance, such as how many hits Billy had, your players will focus on outcomes.

One other thing I will do at the end of both practices and games is something called "raise ups." "Raise ups" are a chance for players to "raise up" a teammate for something they did well—again, always something controllable. The tendency for players is to "raise up" Johnny for his twenty-four points, but we do not want the "raise ups" to be based around hits, points, etc. If Johnny scored twenty-four, he's probably doing just fine mentally. What about Billy, who didn't score any points? Billy played tenacious defense against the other team's best player. Billy can repeat that tenacious play in the next game, because it is controllable.

As you begin each season coaching your son or daughter, be sure to write down the character skills you hope they gain throughout the season. Focus your coaching and your attention on those skills. Helping develop your son's or daughter's (and all your players') character is the number one goal in coaching.

A few months ago, I started working with a college athlete. She struggled with many parts of the mental game. She struggled to bounce back after a mistake. She would get frustrated when her team wasn't playing well. She questioned her place on the team and often wondered if she was good enough to play at this level. She didn't enjoy her successes and saw her mistakes as signs of weakness. We began to talk about character skills. She determined what character skills she valued, why they were important, and the actions she needed to take to drive toward acquisition of these skills. The character skills were resilience, leadership, confidence, and gratitude. She began to focus her thoughts on these skills. She became intentional about directing her actions toward building these skills. At practices, she was mindful of these skills. In the weight room, she directed her actions toward acquisition of these skills. Now these skills are who she has become: resilient, a leader, confident, and grateful.

She has become much stronger mentally. Challenges she faces are met with resilience. Obstacles her team encounters are met by a team unified under a strong leader. Situations that cause self-doubt are met with confidence. She is grateful for her successes and her failures.

Our thoughts drive our actions. Our actions drive our behaviors. Our behaviors drive who we become. Who do you hope your son or daughter becomes?

CHAPTER 12

FINAL THOUGHTS

"You are going to make mistakes, learn from them, and push forward."

— *Lucie Henrich,*
Gustavus Adolphus, Soccer

It has taken me nearly three years to complete this book. In that time, I have watched my oldest son, Will, have what many would consider a successful freshman baseball season at Arizona State University, followed by what many would consider an unsuccessful sophomore season, followed by transferring to the University of Michigan. I have watched my younger son, Drew, commit to Georgia Tech University, lose a heartbreaking game in the Minnesota State Baseball Tournament, win the "Rawlings Gold Glove" for best defensive player, and go hitless at one of the most prestigious high school events of the year. The ups and downs are always part of sports.

Through it all, I know my boys have learned many things. They have learned that hard work pays off, but not necessarily in the ways that you had imagined, and not necessarily in the time frame that you had hoped for. They have learned that resiliency is hard to develop, but it's worthwhile, and it's worth fighting for. They have learned that confidence comes from within, not from what anyone else thinks of them. They have learned the importance of humility, respect, and kindness.

Through all the ups and downs I have always tried to keep my eye on the big picture: what type of men are they becoming? No doubt I have wondered at times if we have steered them in the right direction. If we should have zigged when we zagged. But as I type this now, I can honestly say that I have tried to develop good men. Baseball is no doubt a huge part of our life. Like you, we have invested countless dollars and a huge amount of time in our sport. But what keeps me going, and allows me to sleep at night, is knowing that baseball is just an avenue to building great character.

REFERENCE GUIDE

As I read through this book one final time (for about the twentieth time!), I realize how much information I have covered. Maybe so much information that at this point you feel a little overwhelmed? If so, below is a reference guide that you can call on in a pinch. I hope this guide will provide a quick resource when you, or your son or daughter, have the need for a mindset reboot:

- Focus on the person over the player.
- Focus on the character skills that you, and your son or daughter, think are important.
- Prior to each new season, establish goals with your son or daughter. Be sure that there is an understanding of goals that are controllable vs. uncontrollable. Set character, mental, and physical goals. Revisit the goals throughout the season, especially during times of adversity.
- Adversity is an opportunity to learn and grow.
- Without fun, your son or daughter will invariably lose passion for their sport.
- Intrinsically motivated athletes have the best experience and best performance. In order to feel intrinsically motivated, young athletes need autonomy. Make sure you are allowing your son or daughter enough space to feel a sense of autonomy.

- If your son or daughter is feeling anxious prior to or during a game, it is totally normal. Help them to navigate the anxiety, not ignore it.

I truly hope this book helps you and your son or daughter.

Enjoy the ride!

ABOUT THE AUTHOR

Travis Rogers holds a Master's Degree in Sport and Exercise Science with an emphasis on Sports Psychology from the University of Minnesota. He is the owner of MindRite Training, working with athletes to improve mental performance. He and his wife Nancy have raised two athletic boys (Will is a junior, playing baseball at the University of Michigan, and Drew is a high school senior committed to playing baseball at Georgia Tech University). Travis played baseball collegiately at New Mexico State University and has been a coach for over fifteen years. Travis is passionate about creating an environment within sports that allows a young athlete to maximize their personal and physical development.

Learn more and get resources for this book at: mindritetraining.com/parentingathletickids

www.ingramcontent.com/pod-product-compliance
Lightning Source LLC
LaVergne TN
LVHW041339080426
835512LV00006B/534